Dedication:

DEDICATED to my mom, E
Patton whose love I miss e\   ...gie
day. Thank you for setting such an
excellent example in love, compassion,
kindness and generosity. I strive to be
like you each and every day. I eagerly
look forward to the time when we are
reunited in Paradise on earth.
– Luke 23:43

Special Thanks:

Brendon Burchard, thank you for never
ever giving up on your dream to share
your story and help others. I have never
had the opportunity to meet you, but I
have been a student of yours for many
years. I did get a chance to meet your
mom at one of your events. She is an
amazing woman and I can see why you
turned out to be the man that you are. I
would also like to extend my deepest
condolences for the loss of your father
and grandmother.

Free Online Bonus Masterclass – How to Master Your Mindset & Make Money Online

Get it now at:
http://bit.ly/MyFreeBonus

Copyright 2017 Meiko S. Patton

no responsibility for actions taken or not taken.

A Message from the Author

Thank you for purchasing this book.

Over the next 21 days, I want to introduce you to how the postage stamp has been beneficial in my life and how you can use it to harness your own power. Congratulations on taking the first step.

I know that your time is valuable and that's why I made the chapters short, succinct and to the point. So, do me a favor and commit to reading at least one chapter a day. The key to dramatic success and transformation is persistence and consistency.

But, above all, please be sure to take advantage of my **FREE Online Masterclass – How to Master Your Mindset & Make Money Online**

Details can be found here: http://
http://bit.ly/MyFreeBonus

Table of Contents:

Note to the reader: Story of man in freezer

The following is an excerpt from the introduction of the book, Don't Tell Me It's Impossible Until After I've Already Done It, by Pam Lontos. I read this book many years ago, and Pam's story of transformation and this introduction never left my mind. Here it is:

It was one of those pitch-black nights that the man who worked security at the railroad yard had come to hate. The dark brought uncertainty, a sense of not knowing what waited ahead, and he disliked it passionately – almost as much as he disliked the responsibility of entering the refrigerated railcars used to transport perishable goods. There, the cold turned the dreaded darkness into something almost tangible. Though he admitted it to no one, the cold and darkness terrified him for reasons he could not explain.

He was nearing the welcome end of his rounds and had put off going into the refrigerator car until the last minute. The silent dread weighed on him more heavily than usual as he wearily climbed inside to make sure all was in order.

Then, just seconds before he had completed his duties and would be ready to return to the warmth of his well-lit office, he heard a sound that struck in him a numbing note of terror.

He was aware of what had happened even before shining his flashlight in the direction of the heavily insulated car door. The door had slammed shut, locking him in, alone. He knew the door could not be opened from the inside. And there was no one on the outside to call for help. He was trapped. Doomed.

He would die there, he knew, either from the cold or from lack of air. It was the thought of freezing to death that concerned him most. He screamed until his lungs burned and banged on the door until his hands were swollen and bruised. In time, however, the panic subsided and a resolution unlike any he'd ever felt set in. His situation was hopeless.

He decided his last act would be to record his agonizing death for whoever might eventually find him. Taking a pencil from his jacket pocket, he wrote on the car wall: "It is so cold in here I can hardly stand it…"

After a while he struggled from the corner where he had huddled and wrote a second line: "It's colder still…my fingers are getting numb."

Then, later: "I'm slowly freezing to death…"

And ultimately: "These are probably my last words…"

By the time he had scribbled his final sentence, the writing was almost illegible, the hand of a dying man.

It was the following morning when his body was found, slumped in one corner of the refrigerator car.

The coroner had great difficulty determining the cause of death. There had, he determined, been sufficient ventilation inside the car to allow a man to survive for days. And, since the refrigeration apparatus of the car had been out of order, there was no way the man could have frozen to death.

In fact, the temperature inside the car when it was finally opened was fifty-six degrees.

The moral of the story is clear. The security man, burdened by fears and self-doubts, had become the victim of the awesome power of his subconscious. He *expected* the worst and, unfortunately, saw those expectations realized. Rather than making a positive and optimistic assessment of his situation and seeking some way to get through the nightmare, *he gave up.* He surrendered to a reality that existed only in his mind.

The End.

I mention this story because this man paid the ultimate price. He expected the worst and that is exactly what he got. He gave in to his fears, doubts and insecurities. He gave up on life.

Inside the pages of this book, you will see how I almost gave up as well. But, I know my story is not unique. Many of us have been in the same position that the security guard found himself in, looking at life through negative lenses, giving in to doubt and fear. But I am here to tell you that there is another way. I call it the Postage Stamp Method.

Reflect for a moment on this quote from the book, A Return to Love by Marianne Williamson.

"Our deepest fear is not that we are inadequate. Our deepest fear is that we are powerful beyond measure. It is our light, not our darkness that most frightens us. We ask ourselves, Who am I to be brilliant, gorgeous, talented, and fabulous? Actually, who are you *not* to be? You are a child of God. Your playing small does not serve the world. There is nothing enlightened about shrinking so that other people won't feel insecure around you. We are all meant to shine, as children do. We were born to make manifest the glory of God that is within us. It's not just in some of us; it's in everyone. And as we let our own light shine, we unconsciously give other people permission to do the same. As we are liberated from our own fear, our presence automatically liberates others."

Isn't that powerful?

This book will help you get past the limitations you've been placing on yourself. It will give you a new outlook on life. Your perspective will change. You will want to live each day to the full, if you are not already doing so. You will stop procrastinating, doubting yourself and finally gain the confidence you need. You will no longer allow depression to have the upper hand. You will create bulletproof habits, improve your self-esteem and self-image and truly become happy and fulfilled by serving and creating instead of consuming. As you continue reading this book, you will come to understand that consuming without intention will only leave you feeling stuck, depleted and empty.

Do what author Steven Pressfield suggests in his book, The War of Art. In the last pages of his book, he says that if you don't do the thing you were meant to do, you, not only hurt yourself, you hurt the planet. He says, "Don't cheat us of your contribution. Give us what you got."

So give us what you got and never ever give up.

Chapter 1: Me, Mom & The Postage Stamp

I didn't know it at the time, but 48 hours was all the time that I had left with the most extraordinary woman I had ever known. She had given birth to me in the early 1970s and raised me to be the woman that I am today.

As I reflect back, the night before she died was no different than any other. But the next day and every day since, has never been the same. Mom had now been diagnosed with cancer for the second time in her life. The first time was in the early 1990s and now it was back again, rearing its ugly head, but this time, with a vengeance.

The first time mom was diagnosed, the doctors caught the ovarian cancer in Stage 1. Diagnosis at this stage gave my mom a better chance at survival. She had a hysterectomy and, poof, the cancer was gone. We all were beyond excited and relieved. It never occurred to any of us, that it could ever come back again. When she was diagnosed with Stage 4 colon cancer in 2007, which would eventually metastasize to her liver, it was a devastating blow for our entire family, but, especially to mom.

Mom was born in Mississippi and raised in Cleveland, OH in the 1950s.

Mom was the second eldest of nine children and the only left-handed child. She was very smart, kind and extremely creative. Many nights she would sit with her younger siblings and make up fabulous tales to amuse them. They were always enthralled and intrigued by her amazing storytelling ability. One particular story she conjured up centered around a little girl on her way home. As she was running home, the sun set and she encountered a large obstacle in the middle of the road. What was it? A Giant Strawberry, of course. The strawberry was so large, she couldn't get around it. When my mom told me this story I asked her to please tell me the ending. She told me that was only detail of the story she could remember, so with just that one detail, I made up the remainder of the story and had the children's book, *The Giant Strawberry* published in 2006, in her honor. (**Full Circle Love #2 – mom began the story and I finished it).**

When mom was diagnosed with Stage 4 colon and liver cancer in 2007, she was residing in Atlanta, GA with my older brother. She would eventually fly back to California, where I lived, so I could care for her. I had the awesome privilege of being her primary caregiver until her death. Working full-time for the Postal Service while caring for my dying mother was not easy, but with a lot of prayer, support from friends and having an understanding employer, I was able to care for my mom in the best possible manner.

I am the youngest of three children and the only girl. To say that my life was shattered when my mom died would be an understatement. Whenever I hear of girls that grow up without a close bond to their mothers, my heart goes out to them because my mother was my best friend. She always knew exactly how to answer any question I had and she comforted me whenever I needed it. What I miss the most about mom now are her hugs and hearing her say, "I love you, Meiko." I haven't heard those words, or felt her warm embrace in nearly a decade. Many times throughout the day I feel lost and utterly alone because she is no longer here.

Being the only girl had its advantages. I got the chance to spend a lot of time with my mom and really get to know her as a person a part from her just being my mom. She was the most generous soul you would ever meet. She was always kind and brave and courageous. She told me the following story about her life before she married my dad which exemplifies her bravery. She had two sons by my father while she was still in her early 20s but was not married to him. After her second child, even though she was not religious at the time, she felt deep in her heart that committing fornication was wrong, so she decided to stop having sex until she got married. She wanted to marry mom dad, but he did not feel the same way. Mom was not going to back down from her decision, so, instead of feeling sad or complaining, she made a decision. She had seen commercials about California, so she decided she would move there and start over on her own. She asked her older sister if she wanted to go with her. Her sister, who had four small children at the time, agreed. So mom, and her two sons, along with her sister and her four children took the bus and moved to California in the early 1970s. They did not know a soul there, but they courageously took life by the bootstraps and made a new life for themselves. They were more than courageous, they were fearless, just as Ariana Huffington describes in her book, ***On Becoming Fearless***.

Not too long after my mom arrived in California, the father of her two sons, my dad, wanted to come and join her, he had a change of heart after mom left. Mom had started dating a wonderful new man at the time, but decided to end things with him and give the father of her two children another chance if he promised he would marry her. They got married and I was born shortly thereafter.

You see, mom was a strong and determined woman. She did not let obstacles stop her from accomplishing what she set out to do. I looked up to her as a woman after she told me how she stood her ground and would no longer betray her body, marriage was the only option for her. She will always be my role model in life.

Me

When I was five years old, something devastating happened to me that would change the way I viewed myself and how I related to others, even how I related to my mom.

Prior to this trauma, I was a very outgoing, happy child. But afterwards, I became very inward and withdrawn and shy. I also began to make rude comments to my mother whom I loved, but I didn't know how to process the anger and self-loathing I was feeling as a young, vulnerable child. I wish I would have had the courage to tell my mom that I was violated sexually, but I felt ashamed and didn't know how to put that into words with my five-year-old vocabulary.

Eventually, when I became an adult, I did tell my mom and she held me and cried and apologized for not knowing what happened to me so many years ago. I tell this story because at the time, my mom was the only person I had ever told, so when she died, I lost more than just a mother, I lost my best friend, my confidant, my rock and protector.

I remember watching Oprah one day, she was talking to a child molester who was apologetic for what he had done, but still the damage was done. I remember hearing him say, "The person I molested will never know what sort of person she would have been." That is so true of molestation. It robs you of your innocence. It steals your self-confidence and self-love. It murders who you would have been.

This trauma that I experienced as child was something I had never really dealt with as an adult up until that point, so when mom died, the pain of her death was compounded by the pain of this buried trauma finally coming to the light. It was as if her death had somehow triggered these deeply suppressed memories of my trauma because in my mind she was no longer there to comfort and protect me. The double-pain and self-loathing I felt was so intense that I wanted to die.

That's why I credit the postage stamp with saving my life.

When you think of something saving your life, a postage stamp doesn't exactly come to mind.

You normally think of things like:

- A policeman coming to your aid
- A firefighter rescuing you from a burning building
- A trusted professional you talk to about your recurring thoughts of suicide
- A trusted friend you confide in that is always there when you need them

Several of the above things were true for me too, but what I kept coming back to was the thought of the postage stamp.

The postage stamp helped to reorient my thinking (and later therapy too). The postage stamp allowed me to reframe my negativity. Instead of continuing to feel sorry for myself, I asked, "How can this situation benefit me?"

After contemplating the purpose of the postage stamp, I realized that the only real change I had over my life was over my thoughts and my body. So I made decision, just like my mom did when she came to California.

I knew that mom was a fighter and as her daughter, I wanted to fight as well. When she came to live with me in Los Angeles, she fought every single day of her life. I would take her to the doctor and we would sit all day until she was proscribed her medication. Near the end of her life, she would be in so much pain that she had to take morphine just to get through the day and yet she continued to fight. Mom was an avid reader and she read every medical journal and alternative therapy journal on cancer that she could find. She changed her diet; we started juicing all her vegetables while steadily searching for a cure. We tried everything imaginable from the hyperbaric chamber to alternative medications. Mom fought to the very end, so how could I just give up. I couldn't. I wouldn't, thanks to the postage stamp. In a very remarkable sense, mom was just like the postage stamp.

Chapter 2: Mom & The Postage Stamp

"She's not going to make," screamed the frantic paramedic that rushed into the room where mom was. It was the morning that would change the rest of my life.

A few minutes earlier, I called 911 because now mom was unresponsive. I couldn't believe it. The night before was exactly like every other night. We talked; she was in no more pain than usual. She woke up several times during the night, which was normal and I got up when she did, as I always did, but now that it was morning, she was not responding to my voice. Her eyes had a glaze look about them. She wasn't really making any sounds. I panicked and froze for several minutes. My mind couldn't or wouldn't process what was happening before my very eyes. I wanted to scream, but I couldn't, so I cried as I dialed 911.

Within minutes the paramedics arrived. I told them about her diagnosis and that's when the paramedic shouted the statement above. After she was rushed to the hospital, I learned that she had slipped into a coma. I spoke to the doctor and he explained the situation. He said that they could try to wake her but that she would still be in the same pain she was in before or they could take her off the machine and allow her to slowly die. Basically it was up to me – prolong her life or let her die.

Fortunately, my mother and I had this conversation a few months before she died. It was a difficult conversation to have, but, I told her I would respect her wishes and not prolong her life. The doctor told me to think it over, so I went home and barely slept the whole night. The next day I told the doctor to take her off the machine and within hours she was gone.

The Stamp

So what comes to your mind when you think of a postage stamp?

When I think about it, postage stamps are the ultimate ambassadors for their name country. The postage stamp is the most widely known postal symbol the world over. The postage stamp is well-travelled. It travels from country to country representing the past, present and future of its nation.

The primary function of a stamp is of course, to pay for mail, but if you take the time to really examine a stamp you'll have the opportunity to learn about many subjects on a vast array of topics. You can learn about your family history and even trace your genealogy through postage stamps.

Postage stamps are small in stature but touch every aspect of our society.

What is your favorite postage stamp?

My favorite postage stamp is shown below. It reminds me of giving. Mom was the ultimate giver.

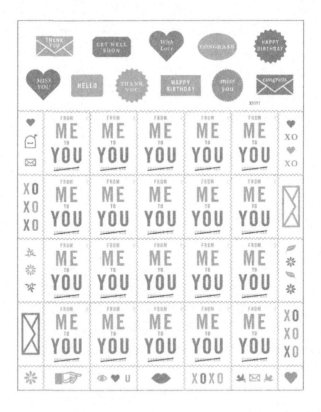

Chapter 3: Full Circle Love

When my mother was diagnosed the second time with cancer, we were still very hopeful that she would survive, optimistic in fact.

Even though she was diagnosed with Stage 4 cancer, we were optimistic that she would beat it again, because she had done it before. Besides, if you knew my mom, then you knew, she was a health queen. She ate vitamins every day, she juiced vegetables, didn't eat a lot of processed foods, she was an all-round healthy person. So not only was this diagnosis hard to take, it blind-sided all of us, but we were determined to fight.

My mom was a fighter and she would not give up without a strenuous fight. From diagnosis to the day my mom died was a total of 9 months. The amount of time it takes to have a baby. The amount of time it took my mom to have me. I point this out because I almost didn't get here.

I mentioned how my mom and dad had just gotten back together. They had just gotten married and now they were striving for the American Dream. They already had two kids, now they were both working to buy a house with that beautifully cliché white picket fence. They were not trying to feed another mouth. So when my mom got pregnant with me she seriously thought about ending my life. She told me years later that she couldn't go through with it because she loved me and wanted me to live just like she let my two older brothers live.

I tell you this story because one of most beautiful things that I got a chance to do was pay-it-forward to my own mother some 30 years later. You see, she took care of me for the first 9 months of my life, while I was growing and developing in her stomach at a time when my life was literally and completely dependent on her and I got the amazing opportunity, some 30 years later to take care of her the last 9 months of her life when she was literally and completely dependent on me. I like to call it full circle love. My mom, as you now know eventually lost her fight with colon and liver cancer.

She succumbed to death on November 17, 2008. *(Full Circle Love #1 – mom cared for me for 9 months in her womb and I cared for mom for 9 months until her death).*

Chapter 4: The Power of a Postage Stamp

At the time of my mom's death, I was understandably numb, because not only was I dealing with her death, but also with my resurfaced childhood trauma. I managed to write the obituary and get things prepared for the funeral service and repass, but after that I completely fell apart.

I was still working for the Postal Service as a Letter Carrier, but about five months later I got a job promotion to San Diego, CA as a Writer/Editor for the Postal Service. It was a much needed change, but even though I was living a beautiful city, I was still a broken person.

I would go to work every day and when I came home I just crawled into bed and cried. On the weekends, I never got out of the bed or even went outside. When Monday rolled around, I repeated the same routine. During this time, I had major thoughts of suicide. I was depressed all the time, but I never let anyone know. I would pray every night not to wake up the next day. But somehow, I kept waking up.

My mom was my best friend and when she died, it was as if I died as well. I couldn't see any point in going on. She was the one person that truly loved me unconditionally and now that love was gone. I felt sad, empty, alone, discouraged, fearful, and every other negative word you can think of. One day my mind was really on this loop about taking my life, I couldn't stop it. But as I was imagining how I would end it all, the thought of the postage stamp entered my brain.

I reflected on the one main purpose of the postage stamp. Yes, it allows your mail to be delivered, but its main purpose is to stick to its recipient until its job is complete. The postage stamp never deviates from its purpose. It has only one goal and it fervently sticks to its goal until it is realized. The postage stamp never gives up. Henry Wheeler Shaw said it best. He said:

"Consider the postage stamp. It secures success through its ability to stick to one thing till it gets there."

That one statement got me to thinking. If the postage stamp has but one purpose in life and it never strays from that purpose, then what was my purpose and why had I strayed? How could I end my life before it had ever begun? How could I end my life before I found my purpose and achieved my goals? How could I just give up?

Over the next several weeks, I would come back to this analogy again and again. It never left my mind. As I began to contemplate my purpose, my thoughts of suicide subsided. I was always an avid reader, so when I read that it only takes 21 days to form a new habit, I decided to do something unheard of. I decided that the one thing I have full control over is my mind and body. Because my mind was moving to more positive things, I decided to do something about my body. I told myself I would get up at 4 am every day and go work out at the gym before work for 21 days.

When I told most people this, they thought I was crazy. But I knew I had to do something drastic – my life depended on it. So I got up every day and worked out before going to work. I liked it so much that I continued doing it after the 21 days. That was in 2009. I later researched and wrote about on Entrepreneur.com how most successful entrepreneurs get up earlier than the average person, so I knew I was on to something. Fast forward to 2017 and I still keep up that same regimen. Yes, people still think I'm crazy, but I know that routine is what saved me among other things.

One of the 'among' other things that helped me was a book, titled, <u>The Depression Cure: The Six-Step Program to Beat Depression without Drugs</u> by Dr. Stephen Ilardi. I came across his book a few years after he wrote it, but the information inside really helped me. The following excerpts below are taken directly from his book.

- <u>Brain Food</u> – He talks extensively about how adding a daily fish oil supplement is one of the most potent ways to fight depression and keep it from coming back

- <u>Don't Think, Do</u> – He states that when we are depressed we tend to dwell on negative things, often replaying them in our minds over and over again. He says when we ruminate in this way, we tend to withdraw, especially socially. That's why it is crucial to find activities to get you moving and connecting socially. Go outside. Go for a walk or a run. Like Nike says, Just Do It.

- <u>Antidepressant Exercise</u> – Exercise is not only good for your physical health, it's equally important for your mental health. Most people forget that. Studies have shown that exercise actually changes the brain. It sharpens memory and concentration and helps us to think more clearly. Aerobic exercise is the most potent antidepressant exercise. It has the ability to reverse the toxic effects of depression on the brain.

- <u>Let there be light</u> – He says, "If you spend most of your time inside, your eyes' light receptors simply aren't getting the stimulation they need. That in turn, can have a major effect on both your brain chemistry and your body clock." Bright light stimulates the brain's production of serotonin. This is a big deal because the amount of serotonin we receive affects our mood and behavior. Thus, bright light ramps up the brains serotonin which causes an antidepressant effect. Light also boosts feeling of well-being. And if you feel you, you're more likely to socialize with others which lifts your depression.

- Get Connected – We are born to connect. It is etched in our DNA. We need other people. When we are deprived of social contact for just a few days, our stress hormones escalate, our mood and energy plummet and other key biological processes quickly begin to decline. Isolation exacerbates depression. Social withdrawal amplifies depression. Conversely, anything that enhances social connectedness helps us fight depression. Ilardi suggests you do three things; 1- Disclose how you feel to a friend 2- Educate your friends about the illness. Depression robs people of their ability to function. 3- Ask for help from a close friend or professional. When you spend time with others, it helps your left frontal cortex to reactivate itself, which provides a direct antidepressant effect.

- Habits of Healthy Sleep – Illardi says, "It is only during sleep that the body and brain have a chance to do their repair work to undo the subtle damage suffered by millions of cells over the course of each day – and to perform a daily tune-up so things continue running smoothly. Sleep is what keeps us firing on all cylinders." Sleep disturbance and depression go hand in hand. Lack of sleep also plays a major role in triggering illness. In the battle against depression, sleep belongs high on the priority list.

I wholeheartedly recommend Dr. Ilardi's book, , The Depression Cure: The Six-Step Program to Beat Depression without Drugs, because it truly helped me. I immediately put all these things into practice. I started eating healthier, I was already starting to exercise, I never had any problem with sleep, but I made sure I got my eight hours every night, I then made sure I went outside to get sunlight.

I bought a Fitbit and that not only helped me walk 10,000 steps a day, but it forced me to get outside and take in the beauty of nature and finally I reconnected with my faith and began fellowshipping with my congregation again on a consistent basis. All those things combined really catapulted me out of my anxious, depressive and suicidal state. But it all started with the thought of the postage stamp and how it never ever gives up, that helped me implement all the other strategies.

Chapter 5: The Emergence of NEGU Academy

After I had time to contemplate what exactly the postage stamp had done for me, I knew that I wanted to share what I had learned to help others. Just to recap, the postage stamp never deviates from its purpose. It has only one goal and it fervently stick to its goal (the letter) until it is realized (delivered). The postage stamp never ever gives up.

The thought of the postage stamp gave me the courage and confidence to act. It made me push myself forward into action. It gave me a framework with which to begin again.

For so long, I had unwittingly, conditioned by brain with the habit of thinking negative thoughts. My thoughts literally encoded negativity into my brain. But when I began to change, then everything changed for me. When I began to reprogram my thinking that depression fog slowly disappeared.

Thinking about the postage stamp was a technique I used to get myself going. I thought, if a postage stamp can do it, then surely I can too. There is a certain resiliency that a postage stamp possesses. The postage stamp has the ability to be resilient toward its goals. In spite of everything thrown at it, it soldiers on in spite of it all. The characteristics of the postage stamp helped me to be more resilient in the face of my struggles, strife, hurt and disappointments.

I learned that physical movement is the most important thing you can do to change your thinking. Because when you move, your physiology changes and when that happens, your mind has no choice but to follow. You must have a bias towards action. When you condition yourself to act, your life will be renewed and you will begin to feel unstoppable.

In his book, Change Your Brain, Change Your Life, Dr. Daniel Amen introduces you to four of the brain systems that are most intimately involved with our behavior. Below is what he says about the brain in his book:

1. Deep Limbic System – At the center of the of the brain, this is the bonding and mood control center. When this part of the brain is not shooting on all cylinders, people struggle with moodiness and negativity.
2. Basal Ganglia – These structures control the body's idling speed. When this part of the brain works too hard, anxiety, panic, fearfulness, and conflict avoidance are often the result. When it is underactive, people often struggle with concentration and fine motor control problems.
3. Prefrontal Cortex – At the front tip of the brain, this is your supervisor, the part of the brain that helps you stay focused, make plans, control impulses and make good or bad decisions. When this part of the brain is underactive, people have problems supervising

themselves and also have significant problems with attention span, focus, organization and follow-through.

4. Cingulate System – This is the part of the brain he calls, the gear shifter. It allows you to shift attention from thought to thought and between behaviors. When this part of the brain is overactive, people have problems getting stuck in certain loops and thoughts of behavior.

Does any of this resonate with you?

Ding, ding, ding…it did for me.

I truly came to see that number four was the culprit for me. I was stuck in negative thought loops. Like going round and round in a merry-go-round, I kept having the same negative thoughts day in and day out. My cingulate system was working abnormally. I was thinking the same thoughts over and over again. My brain was obsessed with the negativity and I couldn't let it go. I learned that physical movement, such as exercise and eating a better diet really made a huge difference.

Other things that helped get me out of the repetitive cycling of thoughts loop was:

- Singing
- Dancing - I love to dance
- Taking a walk
- Praying
- Exercising

In one way or another we are all struggling. I hope by showing you what helped me, it will serve you and let you know that you too can get through it.

Another perk about understanding how my brain dictated my behavior allowed me to see people in a better light. It made me more compassionate. For instance, in traffic, if someone yells at me, I know that it's not me they're really upset with, it's most likely their deep limbic system or basal ganglia that's off kilter. So I brush it off and keep going.

See the unexpected benefits of the postage stamp!

In my research, I also found out that essential oils can also have a huge impact on your mental and emotional state. For instance some essential oils can help alleviate anxiety, depression, insomnia and post traumatic disorder. I bring this up because whatever you can do to improve your health, you should look into it. A postage stamp does everything it can possibly do to reach its destination. You need to do everything you can do as well. A good book to check out is, Essential Oils: Ancient Medicine by Dr. Josh Axe. Another good resource is Dr. Axe's website. Be sure to check it out as well.

The postage stamp really caused me to change my behavior. It encouraged me to act. It made me take back control of my mind. It's hard to change because of how our brains are magnificently designed, but I am here to tell you, that when you push through and you do finally make that change, you gain a certain level of confidence that is unheard of.

That got me to thinking, what if I could start an online academy that helps people in very fundamental areas of their lives so they would never ever give up as well. And so the emergence of NEGU Academy began. It stands for Never Ever Give Up.

I did some research by going onto YouTube and looking at the most watched videos and the life topics that people really need help on. There were a few I could really speak to and teach because of having overcome depression, doubt, procrastination and gaining self-confidence among other things, but I wanted to tackle more topics.

For me, the 21-day challenge that I took to get up in the morning at 4 a.m. and go to the gym, really changed my life. So I wanted to focus on 21 topics in my academy that could help people quickly in about 21 days. Topics that people had already raised their hand and said, I am interested in learning how to better my life in these areas. So as you go through the remainder of this book, that is what you will read about, 21 topics that I needed help with and I wanted to share with you the things I learned. I am an avid reader, so I will refer to numerous books that helped me. In addition, I curated some great information from my mentor Brendon Burchard. Be sure to check out his website and his amazing online courses. If there are more topics you want me to teach, send me an email at: meiko@meikopatton.com

The following headlines have become true for me. I hope the information contained inside this book can help you in some way too:

- How a Postage Stamp Saved My Life
- How a Postage Stamp Inspired Me to Reach My Goals
- How a Postage Stamp Cured My Depression

- How a Postage Stamp Cured My Doubt
- How a Postage Stamp Cured My Anxiety
- How a Postage Stamp Cured My Bad Habit of Procrastination
- How a Postage Stamp Cured My Feeling of Imposter Syndrome
- How a Postage Stamp Cured My Suicidal Thoughts
- How a Postage Stamp Gave Me the Courage to Begin Anew
- How a Postage Stamp Helped Me Gain More Self-Confidence and Catapulted My Self-Esteem

Chapter 6: The Postage Stamp & Goals – The 10-Step Process

Consider the postage stamp. When you think about it, the postage stamp is the ultimate goal achiever. When it is plucked from its sheet and carefully placed onto that envelope, it in effect says, "I will not stop until I reach my goal. I will not look back. I will not falter. I will not second guess. I will reach my destination come what may. I will follow through. I will honor the struggle along the way. I am small and beautiful, yet mighty and bold. I will never ever give up. What about you?

If one of your goals is to be successful in any area of your life or career, the one thing you must to do is become an attractive person.

Author and late motivational speaker Jim Rohn once said, "Success is something you attract by the person *you become*." Rohn of course, isn't referring to external attractiveness, rather the internal kind.

If you want success and all that it brings, you have to **become** a better, more attractive person.

Period.

Rohn continues, "Your level of success will rarely exceed your level of personal development."

You **become attractive by** developing yourself into the person you need *to be* in order to attract, create, and sustain the level of success you want in your life.

How so?

In his book, The Morning Miracle, author Hal Elrod says that we all want "Level 10" success in every area of our lives, such as:

- Health

- Happiness

- Finances

- Relationships

- Career

Yet our level of *personal development* is not currently at a "Level 10". Personal development can be summed up as the following:

- Knowledge

- Experience

- Mindset

- Beliefs

So when Rohn says, "Your level of success will rarely exceed your level of personal development," he means that if your knowledge, experience, mindset and beliefs are not also at a "Level 10", you will never experience "Level 10" happiness in any significant area of your life.

Life will always be a struggle, because, as he states, our outer world will always be a reflection of our inner world. Your level of success or lack thereof will always parallel your level of personal development.

Personal development starts by taking 100 percent responsibility for everything in your life. This includes the level of your achievements, the results you produce or lack thereof, the quality of your relationships, the state of your health, your income, your debts, your feelings, your thoughts and emotions.

That isn't always easy. Why?

Because most of us have been conditioned to blame something outside of ourselves for the parts of our life that we don't like or aren't working. For instance do you blame any of the following people/situations for the setbacks in your life or for not having achieved everything you could've?

- Parents
- Boss
- Friends
- Media
- Coworkers
- Clients
- Spouse
- Children
- Weather
- Economy
- Lack of Money

- Lack of Education
- The President

The list is endless.

"If you want your life to be different, you have to be willing to do something different first."

– Kevin Bracy

Are you willing?

The 10-Step Process

If you are going to be successful in any area of your life, you first have to believe that you are capable of making it happen. I start with this as groundwork because self-esteem is the single most significant key to your behavior. Motivational Speaker Zig Ziglar said, "It's impossible to consistently behave in a manner inconsistent with how we see ourselves." You have to believe you can do it. You have to believe you have the knowledge, skills and abilities to create the results you desire. If you believe you are worthless, you will not be motivated to add value to yourself.

It all comes down to your attitude.

Believing in yourself is an attitude.

In the July 2017 issue of Success Magazine, New York Times Best-Selling Author Ramit Sethi of, I Will Teach You to be Rich shared four things that helped him to believe in himself.

1. Take brutally small steps with a long-term perspective
2. Over prepare like you cannot even imagine
3. Handle naysayers
4. Be mindful of who you surround yourself with

The great part about it is that you have a choice. When you were a kid, you couldn't choose your parents or environment. But now that you are an adult, the choice of how you see and talk to yourself is yours. You must now choose to believe that anything you set your mind to, you can achieve. Ziglar also said, "It's not your aptitude, but your attitude, that determines your altitude." If you will just believe it is possible, then you will do what it takes to bring about your desired result, but if you think it is impossible, you will not do what is necessary, you will continue to get zero results. Because in life, you hit what you aim for, if you aim at nothing, you will hit it every time. So now, I hope I have you convinced that you have to believe in order to achieve. As Marie Forleo says, "Everything is figureoutable." Yes, believe in your abilities to figure things out.

Step 1: Examine Your Self-Talk

"You are the most influential person you will talk to all day"

– Zig Ziglar

If I was to record how you talk to yourself all day, would I be pleased at how thoughtful and loving you are to yourself? Or would I hear you berate and tear yourself down all day?

Whether you know it or not, you have a running conversation with yourself all day, every day. Do you encourage or criticize yourself? Are you positive or negative with yourself? How you talk to yourself really does make a difference because if you want to change your life, you have to change not only the way you think about yourself, but more importantly, how you *talk* to yourself.

If you have someone in your life that constantly encourages you, that's terrific. But even if you do or don't, you need to become your own cheerleader. You need to become your own encourager. Stop and think, have you ever complimented someone? I'm guessing yes. Now, have you ever complimented yourself on how you look, feel, on a job well-done? Don't just recognize other people, recognize you. Start speaking positively and consolingly to yourself. When you make a mistake, don't berate yourself, just tell yourself you will do better next time and you are gaining valuable experience.

Step 2: Banish your Limiting Beliefs

"When a man has put a limit on what he will do, he has put a limit on what he can do."

– Charles Schwab

The greatest prison is the prison we create for ourselves. When we tell ourselves that we can't do something or we are not good enough or worthy, this distances us from our true value and worth as a human being. You are worthy simply because you exist.

In the book, Success Principles, Jack Canfield outlines four steps to transforming your limiting beliefs into empowering ones.

1. Identify a limiting belief

2. Write down how the belief limits you

3. Decide how you want to be, act, feel

4. Create a turnabout statement that affirms or gives you permission to be, act or feel this way

Step 3: Develop A Positive Attitude

"Every man is where he is by the law of his being; the thoughts he has built into his character have brought him here."

- James Allen

According to psychologist Sydney Jourard, 85 percent of your success in work is determined by your attitude and personality.

In his book, As A Man Thinketh, James Allen says we do not attract what we want, but rather we attract who we are, for we are the sum total of our thoughts.

A positive mental attitude affects your outlook on life which in turn affects your behavior.

Our minds are extraordinarily powerful. Your thoughts control and determine almost everything that happens to you. Our thoughts can either make us happy or sad. That's why developing a positive mental attitude is so important. Our thoughts trigger images, pictures and emotions that can either make us dwell on success and confidence or the exact opposite. For whatever we think and believe with conviction will become our reality.

It has been said that the world is a living expression of how you are using and have chosen to use your mind. So protect it at all costs. Never finish a negative sentence. Don't dwell on negative things. Dwell only on good and good will follow.

Step 4: Add Value

"People who add value to others do so intentionally. I say that because to add value, leaders must give of

themselves and that rarely occurs by accident."

-John Maxwell

One of the quickest ways to change your negativity into positivity is to add value or simply help someone else. Making a difference in the life of someone else invariably lifts your own self-esteem. It's difficult to feel bad about yourself when you're doing something nice for someone else. There is also a reciprocal effect.

When you add value to others, they value you more. So you get to have more love in your life. That's the beauty in giving. When you give to others, you benefit. The famous scripture is true, "There is more happiness in giving." I heard someone once say, "Whatever you want in life, give to others." If you want more love in your life, then be more loving to others. If you want more support. Be more supportive to others. If you want more understanding, be more understandable with others. It's really that simple.

Step 5: Always Do The Right Thing

"I follow three rules: Do the right thing, do the best you can, and always show people you care."

- Lou Holtz

Since your self-worth is based upon positive habits, actions and decisions, you most definitely want to stay away from the feeling of guilt. You can do this when you make a commitment to always do what's right, even if it's difficult. When you feel guilty about something, it harms your self-image and self-esteem.

Conversely, when you do the things that are right, you continue to build character, the same way you play Jenga. You are building blocks that constantly elevate your self-image. You become a stronger and more positive person.

Step 6: Take 100-percent responsibility for your life

"In one of my recent books, 'The Success Principles,' I taught 64 lessons that help people achieve what they want out of life. From taking nothing less than 100 percent responsibility for your life to empowering others, these are the fundamentals to success - and to great leadership."
– Jack Canfield

If you want to be successful, you will have to lose the "blame-game" mentality. You know what I mean, right? If your relationships aren't going the way you want, you can't blame the other person, you have to take full responsibility.

If your health isn't good, you can't blame anyone, you've decided what to eat, so you must take full responsibility. If you are in debt, you can't blame the economy, you have to take 100-percent responsibility for the financial state you're in. I know this isn't easy, but it's a must if you want to be successful.

Oh, by the way, this also goes for complaining. No more of that either because when you complain, you are blaming other people. You are the common denominator in your life, so that means you are the cause of all your life experiences.

If you add 2 plus 2 and get 5, is it the fault of mathematics? No, it's YOU. If you are not getting the results you want in life, it's not because of something outside yourself, it's YOU. You are the problem, but fortunately, you are the solution as well. So no more lame excuses, ok?

If something doesn't go as planned, ask, "How did I create or contribute to this? What can I learn from this? How can I avoid this outcome in the future? The truth is that, you either create or allow everything that happens to you. You create it by your actions. You allow it by your inactions, or in other words, your unwillingness to change. When you fully understand this, you will come from a place of power and make the changes that need to be made.

Step 7: Decide Exactly What You Want

"The world has a habit of making room for the man whose words and actions show that he knows where he is going".

– Napoleon Hill

In order to attain professional achievement, you must decide what you really want from your life and career. Take a minute to identify what you love doing. What is your passion? Look deep inside yourself to determine what you really enjoy.

It's simple. All of us have a gift. Determine whatever it is you enjoy doing that takes the least amount of effort. Now write it down.

Think back over your past jobs. What have been your most satisfying experiences and your most enjoyable moments?

Your aim is to replicate those feelings as you either embark on a new career or entrepreneurial endeavor. But you must first accept the responsibility of deciding what you want and then dedicating yourself to becoming the person you need to be in order to get where you want to go.

One technique that many use with great success is visualization. Visualization is the act of seeing yourself where you want to be in 'x' number of years.

For instance, in three years, where do you want to be career wise? What is your ideal job, your ideal salary and your ideal working conditions? Imagine that every job in the world was open to you. What would you enjoy doing day after day? It has often been said that if you find a job that you love to do, you won't really have to work a day in your life. Find your passion and this could be true for you too.

Step 8: Get Clear on Your Why

"There are two great days in a person's life - the day we are born and the day we discover why."

- William Barclay

We often see celebrities that have reached the pinnacle of their industry receiving awards and accolades, but then we will see that same celebrity the next day sometimes getting arrested.

Why the discrepancy?

Their focus on succeeding in one area of life created a great imbalance with the other areas. You do not want to be like this. You want balance in every area of your life.

Strive for congruency.

Becoming successful is great, but make sure you do not focus all your attention on this to the detriment of your health and relationships with others. Get clear on exactly why you want what you want. Jim Rohn said," Beware of who you become in pursuit of what you want." Without a purpose, you can easily become lost. Start by figuring out what your core values are.

All companies have clear, written values or mission statements that keep them on course. What is your personal mission statement? Just as companies thrive when they know where they are going, individuals do too. You can improve your personal and by extension your professional life by deciding what your core values are and not deviating from them.

When you are clear on your 'why', the 'how' becomes easier to see.

Step 9: Invite Pain over for Dinner

"The greater danger for most of us is not that our aim is too high and we miss it, but that it is too low and we reach it."

- Michelangelo

Take out a piece a paper and pencil. Draw two dots, one on the far right and the other on the far left. Then draw a line to connect the two dots. The dot on the left represents where you are and the dot on the right represents where you want to be. That long line in the middle represents a gap.

How can you bridge this gap?

You can do so with new knowledge and updated skills. You will have to do something new and different to get to where you want to be. But it won't be easy though because anything worthwhile never is.

Just look around you. Everything you see began as a thought in someone's mind. The chair you're sitting on. The book you're reading. The car you drive. The clothes you're wearing. Everything begins with a thought. Then that thought turned into action. Action is oftentimes accompanied with pain. Why? Because you have to do something different. You have to get out of your comfort zone. You have to have self-discipline.

Olympic Gold Medalist Michael Phelps trained for years to get to the pinnacle of his sport. Olympic Gold Medalist Gabby Douglas did too. It wasn't easy, but they were dedicated and stuck to a rigorous training schedule every day.

If you want similar results in your professional life, you have to be willing to put in the time. If you really want to be successful in life, you have to be willing to suffer a little pain in the process. But the great thing about pain is that it's only temporary but the benefits can last a lifetime.

Step 10: Think your way to Success

"All that a man achieves or fails to achieve is the direct result of his thoughts."

– James Allen

In his book, Make Today Count, author John Maxwell list 11 ways of thinking, but the one I want to discuss with you is number seven on his list. It is reflective thinking.

Reflective thinking is the ability to revisit the past in order to gain a true perspective and think with understanding. Why is this so important?

Because reflection can help you achieve better results. I love to write, so I have written down the obstacles I faced and correspondingly, the lessons I've learned from those challenges. It was only by reflecting, that I was able to grow as a person. I saw where I needed to improve my character and I made the needed changes. As a result, I was able to land my dream job for the federal government in 2009. Had I not reflected, I might still be in the same job today.

Reflection allows difficult experiences to be our teachers. If we reflect on the lessons learned you will not only live a better life, but you will be able to implement changes in your life to ensure you do not have to repeat that same experience again. And once you have learned the lesson, you are in a better position to be able to spare someone else those hard life lessons by mentoring others with the wisdom you've gained.

What truly caused me to reflect on my life and the many lessons I learned was the death of my mother. She was a gem of a person and I learned how to be a beautiful caring woman because of her. Since losing her I find myself reflecting on the many things she taught me.

I sit and think of the lessons I learned. I try to help others by dispensing some of her wisdom to them. This reflection has not only helped me personally, but professionally as well.

What will reflective thinking do for you?

And there you have my 10-step process for designing a life you love. If you want to go deeper on these 10 steps, sign up for my academy training here: http://bit.ly/MyFreeBonus

Chapter 7: The Postage Stamp & How Incredibly Successful People Think

Consider the postage stamp. If you want to be world-class, you have to start thinking like a postage stamp. It never gives up and it never takes the easy route. It masters its mindset because you can't master life until you master your mind.

How would you answer the following questions:

1. I wish I had fewer problems in life. Agree or Disagree

2. I wish I didn't have to struggle so much in life.　　Agree or Disagree
3. I wish I had the opportunities that other people have.　　Agree or Disagree.

If you agreed to any one of the above statements, then you are not thinking like an incredibly successful person.

Success leaves clues. So what clues can we glean from incredibly successful people?

Let's break down each of the foregoing questions.

#1 – I wish I had fewer problems in life

You learn some of the best lessons in life from struggles. So instead of wishing things were easier for you, become better. Learn what you need to learn to overcome the challenges in your life. Then teach what you know to others.

The only way you grow in life is when you face our problems head on. Stop wishing for fewer problems. Whatever you focus on grows, so instead of focusing on your problems, focus on the solutions. A great way to do that is by becoming more skillful. Get useful advice from a mentor. Attend that seminar. Make the needed changes.

Iron is sharpened when it is refined by fire. Challenges will sharpen you when you learn how to cope with them. The best way to cope is to gain wisdom. Wisdom will help you defeat challenges and enable your growth.

Incredibly successful thinkers are a lot like Abraham Lincoln.

Abraham Lincoln – 16th President of the United States

Born into poverty, Abraham Lincoln struggled to overcome every setback in his life. His mother died while he was young. He accumulated debt and struggled to pay it back. Lincoln ran for office and lost more than once. A fiancée died, prompting a nervous breakdown.

Still Lincoln did not give up. Finally he ran for president of the United States -- and, of course, you know the rest. Lincoln failed numerous times but did not stay down in defeat. He learned, pivoted and is remembered as one of the best presidents in history.

If all those setbacks did not face Lincoln, would he have known how strong he really was? Most of us have no idea of what we are capable of until we have no choice but to be that way.

#2 - I wish I didn't have to struggle so much in life

Incredibly successful thinkers are a lot like Helen Keller.

Helen Keller – Author and Crusader

If there was one person who really had to struggle it was Helen Keller.

Born blind and deaf, she never gave up. To her life was either an adventure or nothing at all. She said, "The world is full of suffering, it is also full of the overcoming it." She went on to become an author, lecturer and activist.

If she could overcome her struggles, what about you?

New York Times Best-selling Author Brendon Burchard says, incredibly successful people make it their job to go learn what they don't know. "They take their current limitation and put it on their agenda as a job to do, as a thing to figure out, as something to make happen."

It all starts with your mindset. Our feelings and thoughts create the circumstances in our lives. If your thoughts are negative, you will not achieve success, it's that simple.

If you can master your psychology, the way Helen did, then you can master how incredibly successful people think.

Name one successful person that did not struggle in their life. Exactly, there are none. In order to reach the summit of the mountain, the prerequisite is the valley. If you want to reach the top, you must go the lows of the valley.

If you picked up football and ran across the goal line, would it be a touchdown? No. The touchdown only comes when you are facing a fierce opponent on the field. Only when there is a struggle to win.

Who would David be without Goliath?

Who are you shaping up to be if you only have an easy going, pain-free life?

#3 – I wIsh I had the opportunities that other people have.

There are only two ways in which change happens in your life. Either you create something new in your life or something new will come to you without you having to work at it all. Which one do you have control over?

Yes, incredibly successful people don't wait for circumstances to come looking for them, they go out and find it, no matter how long it takes. Opportunities in life are created by the incredibly successful thinker.

Incredibly successful people like Thomas Edison.

Thomas Edison – Inventor

Where would any of us without the lightbulb? Suffice it to say, all us are immeasurably grateful that Edison did not give up after the struggle. It has been estimated that he failed over 1,000 times before he created the lightbulb. Now, what if he just stopped trying, or what if he just kept wishing that had the opportunities that the wealthy have?

Each so-called failure got him one step closer to the real thing. As Jim Rohn said, "Don't wish it was easier, wish you were better." Keep trying until you succeed. You must not give in to defeat. Each challenge in our life is an experience to learn from and grow from. If there is no friction in your life, you will not grow. Whatever does not grow, dies, just look at the common house plant. If it does not get the water it needs it will cease to exist. If we have no struggle in our life, we will cease to exist as well. Don't wish for more opportunities, go out and develop more skills.

Abraham Lincoln, Heller Keller and Thomas Edison didn't know they had what it took to succeed in life, until they were forced to test their inner strength. New doors open in life only after you rise from a previous defeat and begin to walk anew. When you refuse to let failures hinder your progress, you will eventually arrive at your new destination.

And there you have it. If you want to go deeper with me on this subject, sign up for my academy training here: http://bit.ly/MyFreeBonus

Chapter 8: The Postage Stamp & How to Finally Overcome Fear

Consider the postage stamp. It travels to far and distant lands. It leaves its family (the rest of the book of stamps it was plucked from) and it never sees them again. I'm sure that is fearful for the stamp, but it knows that it has a job to do. It stares fear in the face and forges on. If the postage stamp can do it, you can too. One of my favorite online educators is Brendon Burchard. I refer to him often in this book. Check out his website at: www.brendon.com

When we are born, we have no fears. As we grow we learn and develop fears. The two major fears we learn are the fear of failure or loss and the fear of criticism and rejection. We soon begin to believe that we are inadequate, weak and unlovable. As a result of the destructive criticism and rejection we received in childhood, we hold ourselves back as adults. We sell ourselves short. We quit before we even try. But if we challenge and change our beliefs about ourselves, we can literally transform our lives.

One way to overcome your fear is to define your fear. When we face new situations in life, we normally imagine the worst-case scenario. But, did you know that you can dramatically shrink your fears by simply putting them into words on a piece of paper?

Secondly, accept the challenges that fear presents to you. Instead of shrinking back and giving fear the upper hand, accept fear as a normal part and life and act in spite of it. A great new tool from author and speaker Mel Robbins of The 5 Second Rule, really works. Try it. When you want to do something, just count backwards 5-4-3-2-1 and then do the thing that scares you. Eleanor Roosevelt said, "Do one thing every day that scares you."

Next, think of the benefits of acting in the face of your fear. Think of what it will do for your self-esteem and self-confidence. A good exercise is to physically write down the benefits you will gain by forging ahead. The thing to remember is that every decision you make is helping to form the person you are becoming. Do you want your fear to define you or do you want to take that scary risk and come off the victor?

My online mentor, New York Times Best Selling Author Brendon Burchard, says fear is simply the bad management of your own mental faculties, meaning you continually replay in your mind possible fearful outcomes that might happen one day. Fear manifests itself in what psychologists call the competence confidence loop. When you are not competent in an area, you lack confidence. But, the more you understand something the more confidence you will have in that area. Fear comes from not having that competence and confidence.

Burchard goes further by breaking fear down into three categories which all relate to pain:

1. Loss Pain

2. Process Pain

3. Outcome Pain

Embrace and confront your fears

#1 Loss Pain

The first is loss pain, which happens when you're afraid to move ahead because you fear you'll lose something valuable in the process of trying.

This could manifests itself in a number of ways. For Burchard, he wanted to strike out on his own as an entrepreneur, but if he did, he might lose the security of his full-time job, he would lose his 401k, he would lose that steady paycheck. All that possible loss adds up to fear and for some people, they would rather stay put than to risk suffering loss pain.

But instead of focusing on what you will lose, flip the script and focus on what you will gain. You will gain freedom from a job you may not like, freedom of your time and the ability to earn more than you could ever earn in a 401k. You will also gain challenges, but challenges are good because every challenge stretches and grows you as a person. Remember what you focus on, you feel. What you feel, you will act on.

#2 Process Pain

The second is process pain, which inevitably occurs every time you try something new. You have to go through the process of learning to deal with it. Let's face it, doing something new is hard. You have no competency in what you are learning and sometimes that fear is enough to stop you in your tracks and make you not want to change.

But part of the mastery of life is to see change as something to look forward to, not as something to distance ourselves from. All your life you have avoided change. Tell me, where has that gotten you? See change as an exciting journey to be embarked upon. See all the fun, exciting things that change can bring into your life such as new experiences, new people and a new outlook.

#3 Outcome Pain

The last is outcome pain. This involves not getting the outcome you desired. Of all the three, I think this is the scariest because the what if's begin. What if you overcome loss pain and move ahead and you tackle process pain and bulldoze ahead and in the end you still are no better off than you were when you first began. What if you don't earn more money, what if you don't lose the weight, what if...?

The what-if's get people stuck. They fear the negative what-if's, so they don't try. But try thinking about the positive what-if's. What if once a day, every day, you visualized what your life would be like if, you did this thing you want to do. Visualize how powerful you would feel, how satisfied, how competent, how confident you would be. Think in terms of positive outcomes, not the negative pain.

Burchard insists that people need to overwhelm their fears. Just as an army invades its enemy from every side, a person should do the same with fear, attacking it from every side, as if going to war, because in a sense, you are.

Make this the demarcation line. Resolve to stop suffering in your mind. Ask yourself the hard question, "What do I really want in my life? Why have I not been progressing up to this point in my life?

Take some time to think, meditate and for the first time, focus on the gains and not the losses, the joys and not the sorrows, the positive outcomes and not the negative ones.

And there you have it. If you want to go deeper with me on this subject, sign up for my academy training here http://bit.ly/MyFreeBonus

Chapter 9: The Postage Stamp & How to Deal with a Difficult/Mean Boss or Bully

Consider the postage stamp. When it's placed on a mail piece, it will be grouped with many other mail pieces. Sometimes mail pieces get stuck together as they go through various mail processing machines and the stamps rub each other the wrong way. They peacefully solve their conflict so they can reach their destination.

So just how do you deal with a difficult boss or any person in general?

Well, the good thing is that a difficult or mean person has learned this type of behavior and fortunately, anything learned can be unlearned. And even if your boss doesn't change, you have the power to change yourself and how you view your situation.

First, keep your cool and don't give in to rage. When your temper is out of control, you unwittingly give the difficult person power over you. You are allowing them to dictate your behavior. In that moment, they have control over your emotions, you don't.

Secondly, put all thoughts of revenge out of your mind. Revenge oftentimes backfires and it is not satisfying. Again, this is not who you are, so don't allow someone to make you act in a way that is not true to your character.

Next, if you sense that the situation is getting heated, quickly walk away. Do not get into a shouting match with your employer. Try taking a deep breath, count backwards and simply walk away.

When you are in a more calm state, see if you can talk to your employer and express how you feel. If your boss doesn't listen, you may need to talk to someone higher up in your company. You have the right to be treated with dignity and respect. You are a valuable human being. Above all, never ever give up hope that things will get better.

And there you have it. If you want to go deeper with me on this subject, sign up for my academy training here: http://bit.ly/MyFreeBonus

Chapter 10: The Postage Stamp & The Power of Habit to Get Everything You Want in Life

Consider the postage stamp. It has one singular goal. It remains focused. This focus was a habit it developed in the face of fear. The fear of leaving its home and its other family of stamps, but it knows that in order to get what you want out of life, you must push through in order to create the life you want, and not just settle for the life that is given to you. Let's face it, trying to replace bad habits with good ones is not easy, but it is surely worth it.

Be Realistic

It can be tempting to try to change everything in your life immediately. You tell yourself, 'This week I'm going to stop smoking, stop swearing, stop staying up too late at night, start exercising, start eating better, and start calling my parents.' But trying to reach all your goals at the same time is a sure way to reach *none* of them!

WHAT YOU CAN DO

Work on your habits in realistic
increments. The following steps may
help:

1.   Create two lists—a list
of *good* habits that you would like to
build and a list of any *bad* habits that
you need to get rid of. Do not limit
yourself; on each list, write down as
many as you can think of.
2.   Prioritize the items on your lists,
numbering them in the order of
importance to you.

3.   Choose a few habits—even just
one or two—from each list, and focus
on those. Then move on to the next
one or two habits on each of your lists.

Speed up the process by replacing a
bad habit with a good one. In his
book, Rich Habits - The Daily Success
Habits of Wealthy
Individuals, Tom Corley outlines several
habits that distinguish successful

individuals. Some of those habits as outlined in his book are:

1. Successful people form daily good habits and follow these good habits every single day.

2. Successful people set goals and create a plan to reach those goals.

3. Successful people devote time each day to self-improvement.

4. Successful people manage their consumption of food and engage in regular exercise.

5. Successful people foster, grow and improve their relationships with others every day.

6. Successful people do everything in moderation. No extreme behaviors.

7. Successful people do not procrastinate and have "Do It Now" mindset.

8. Successful people engage in rich thinking every day. They are positive and enthusiastic.

9. Successful people pay themselves first by putting ten percent of their salary into savings and retirement plans.

10.   Successful people are the masters of their thoughts and emotions.

In his book, Corley invites you to take out a sheet of paper and list your bad habits in one column and then invert each one to place under a new column for good habits. It should look like this:

Bad Habit/Good Habit

I watch too much TV.   I limit myself to one hour of TV per day.

I don't remember names.   I write down names and remember them.

Then for 30 days, follow the guidance of your new good habits list. You'll be amazed at how much you can accomplish.

Next, make it *harder to* do the wrong thing. For example, in sticking with our television scenario, if you want to watch less TV, keep the TV unplugged and put it far out of reach, that way when you are tempted to watch more of it than you should, you won't feel like it because of all the extra effort that will be required.

The next step, is to make it *easier **to*** do the right thing. For instance if you plan to exercise first thing in the morning, set your exercise clothing next to your bed the night before. The easier it is to get started, the more likely you are to follow through.

Set up triggers

According to my mentor, Brendon, when it comes to mastering and maintaining good habits, the best thing to do is to set up triggers. He calls it trigger moments.

He gives the following scenario on his website.

Let's say you want to become a **better person.** You want to become more kind, more patient, more loving with people.

Now, you can just set that intention or write that down in your journal or set up on a vision board that you look at once in a while, but in day-to-day life, it's not *enough.*

You need things to trigger you, to remind you to be that particular kind of person.

Brendon suggests that you use your alarm on your phone to help set up these triggers in your life. Simply set up on your phone three alarms during the day with a label that say whatever it is you want to change such as:

- *Close your eyes, take ten deep breaths in, and remind myself to be calm*
- *Be compassionate, patient and kind*

- *Go for a 10-minute walk*

As you go through your hectic day, you might forget to put these new habits into practice, but as soon as your alarm goes off, you'll grab your phone to quiet it and you will see the labels prompting you to do the habits you want to do. Then it happens again and again all throughout the day. These triggers are helping you to actually become the person you to be.

These trigger moments will remind you throughout your day to enact that new behavior. Another trigger Brendon uses is called the **doorframe trigger.** This trigger happens whenever you walk into a new room that has a doorframe. A trigger goes off in your mind that you've associated with that doorframe.

You can use this doorframe trigger when you walk into your office or into any room you walk into. As soon as you do, those three words will be triggered in your mind.

If you do this enough times on a continual basis, you will stick to your habits even more.

"What are the trigger moments you could set up during the day to keep you on track?"

And there you have it. If you want to go deeper with me on this subject, sign up for my academy training here: http://bit.ly/MyFreeBonus

Chapter 11: The Postage Stamp & How to Think Positively

Consider the postage stamp. After it is placed on a mail piece, it never doubts itself. It knows that without a doubt it will arrive at the destination it is bound for. Negative thoughts do not dominate the postage stamp. It always thinks positively. How can you imitate the postage stamp in this instance?

Thoughts are things.

Thoughts lead to feelings.

Feelings lead to actions.

Actions lead to results.

No thought lives in your head rent-free. Each thought you have will either be an asset or liability. It will either move you toward happiness and success or away from it. It will either empower you or weaken you. That's why it's of utmost importance to choose your thoughts wisely in your personal life as well as in your professional life.

If you believe it is possible, it will be possible for you. But if you think it will never happen, then guess what, it won't. Throughout the day, be conscious of your self-talk. Do you talk to yourself in a gentle and loving manner or do you berate yourself every time something goes wrong?

Speak to yourself in a way that conveys that you are a unique person with special talents and abilities. Your combination of education, experience, knowledge, problems, successes, and challenges make you truly remarkable. There's no one else like you. You have great potential, you just have to believe it.

If you have constant negative thoughts recurring in your mind, then it is time to take charge. You need to become the master of your mind and not a slave to it.

Let's talk about how your thoughts are generated. Psychologist says we have two types of thoughts, automatic thoughts and the ability to create our own thoughts and behaviors. Most of what we do is automatic, such as waking up in the morning, getting ready for work, driving to work, etc.

But in order to gain mastery over your life, you must learn to discipline yourself and create your own thoughts. You do this by asking yourself:

- What am I thinking about?
- How am I feeling?

- Why am I thinking this?
- Why am I feeling this way?
- What am I focused on right now?
- Are my thoughts supporting me?
- Are my thoughts hindering me?

Start paying attention to your thoughts so you can change and redirect them. If you are focused on the negative, visualize the positive, the exact opposite of what you are obsessing about. Force your mind to dwell on the positive.

Then, in your mind list 5 things you are grateful for. Repeat these things to yourself throughout the day. Keep doing this until you conquer your negative thoughts.

If you can focus on getting more attentive to what you're feeling and then focusing on what you are grateful for, you will start thinking more positively about life.

One thing I know for sure is that when you take action in life, you move the needle exponentially. Consistent action teaches your mind that you are in control of your brain and your life. So don't be afraid to take these bold actions. Start questioning why you are thinking or feeling a certain way. Behave in a positive way and you will begin to think and act more positively.

And there you have it. If you want to go deeper with me on this subject, sign up for my academy training here: http://bit.ly/MyFreeBonus

Chapter 12: The Postage Stamp & How to Kill Procrastination

Consider the postage stamp. Once it's placed on a letter, it does not hesitate to do its job. It does not hold back. It never slacks off its job. It doesn't wait for the best weather in order to reach its destination. Through rain, sleet and snow, the postage stamp continues to deliver.

Have you ever heard of the Zeigarnik Effect?

Basically it says that thing undone, will plague you forever until you do it. Human nature is to finish what we start and if it is not finished, we experience some type of discomfort. This discomfort manifests itself in different ways.

It usually shows up in your life as procrastination, resistance and fear. In the book *The War of Art* author Steven Pressfield says, "Procrastination is the most common manifestation of resistance because it's the easiest to rationalize. We don't tell ourselves, "I'm never going to write that book." Instead we say, "I'm going to do it tomorrow." And tomorrow never comes.
When it comes to fear, Pressfield says, "Resistance has no strength of its own. Every ounce of juice it possesses comes from us. We feed it with power by our fear of it. Master that fear and we conquer resistance."

The bottom line is that we have to produce in order to be happy. Said another way, if you desire happiness, you must create.

According to Jim Rohn, we must labor. Why does a mother go through the pain and labor to have a child? Because she knows what the outcome will be. New life only comes through labor. Labor produces life. Sure, it might be painful, but we do not get a miracle without it. Don't be afraid of a little pain. It only lasts a short while and you gain so much from it. Honor the struggle.

So, unless you put that good idea into labor, it will work no miracle. You must write that book, compose that song, start your business. You must labor in order to be happy.

The greatest source of unhappiness is self-unhappiness. When you are not happy with who you are. When you know you are doing less than you could do and you don't feel that good about yourself. Do you recall the Bible character Judas. He was the one that betrayed Jesus for 30 pieces of silver. He got the money, a success story, right? Wrong, he later committed suicide. Why? Because he was unhappy with himself. He felt guilt over what he had done. Don't let this happen to you.

Now is the time to act, to produce, to create, to labor. Not tomorrow, not next week, now!

"Life lived for tomorrow will always be just a day away from being realized," said Leo Buscaglia. You need today to be every day. You will never change your life until you change something you do daily. Make today that day. Change one thing that moves you closer to realizing your goals, dreams, and desires.

When you do the right thing every time, even if it isn't easy, you slay procrastination every time. Besides giving yourself a great self-image, every time you choose to do the easy thing, instead of the right thing, you are shaping your identity. In essence you are becoming the type of person who does what's easy, rather than what's right.

On the other hand, when you choose to do the right thing, like sit down at the computer and start writing that great American novel, you are becoming the type of person that follows through on commitments. You are developing personal power and extraordinary discipline.

Everything in our lives are related, yes everything is connected. Every thought you have is a step in one direction or another. Each choice you make has a real impact on the person you are becoming, which ultimately determines where you'll live, where you'll work and what type of car you'll drive. For what shows up in our lives is a direct reflection of our inner thoughts and emotions.

If you allow procrastination and fear to dominate your thoughts, you will only attract more things in your life to validate your thoughts. We get what we focus on. If we focus on lack, scarcity will show up. But if we focus on abundance, riches will appear. To understand that your thoughts are things, there is an experiment in the book E-Squared, by author Pam Grout that proves that every thought has an energy wave that affects everything else in the universe. That's why you can't afford yourself the luxury of a negative thought.

Another reason to banish negative thoughts is outlined, in the book, Feelings Buried Alive Never Die, by author Karol Truman. She says, "A growing body of evidence indicates that virtually every ill that can befall the body – from acne to arthritis, headaches to heart disease, cold sores to cancer – is influenced, for better or worse, by our emotions. Our experiences in life are actually our own state of mind being projected outward." Our bodies are a living canvass of how we feel about ourselves. If our attention is on fear, we are focused on fear and we will inevitably get more things to be fearful of in our life.

To grow, you must take action. In the book, The Depression Cure, author Stephen Ilardi says, "By simply engaging in activity, any activity, we can change the brain in a way that helps reverse depression." If activity helps the brain that is depressed, what can taking action do for you?

Strength can only be developed by effort and practice. You must practice your craft and perfect it. Only then can you overcome procrastination, resistance and fear.

And there you have it. If you want to go deeper with me on this subject, sign up for my academy training here: http://bit.ly/MyFreeBonus

Chapter 13: The Postage Stamp & How to Slay Doubt

Consider the postage stamp. The postage stamp never ever doubts its ability to reach its destination. If it did, you would never receive that package you purchased on Amazon. The postage stamp slays doubt each and every day. How can you act more like the postage stamp in this area?

One day you think you are in good health. The next day you feel ill. Suddenly, you have no strength or vitality. Your head aches and your body is racked with pain. What has happened? Dangerous pathogens have breached your body's defense systems and have attacked vital organs. Left untreated, these invading organisms may destroy your health permanently—even kill you.

The same danger is imposed by insidious doubts.

- We doubt if we are capable.
- We doubt if we are worthy.
- We doubt if we will succeed.
- We doubt if we deserve it.
- We doubt if we are liked.
- We doubt if we are loved.
- We doubt our own voice.
- We doubt our existence.
- We doubt ourselves.

This is an enemy that must be slayed. Don't let doubt stop. You must probe deeper. To slay doubt, you must get to the root of the problem, not simply ignore the symptoms. You cannot simply avoid the problem. Self-doubt is two-sided, on one side is avoidance and on the other side is action. You must act, because when you do, doubt is minimized. You have to condition yourself to act. Once again doubt is a choice. We choose doubt when we fail to act.

So ask yourself, "For what reason am I doubtful?"

We are doubtful because the insidious pathogen of fear spread in your body and breached your defense systems. This occurred because either somebody planted it there, by a thoughtless comment or remark at some point in your life or you cultivated it by your own negative thoughts.

The one way you overcome doubt is to develop stronger faith.

Webster's Dictionary defines faith as complete trust or confidence in someone or something. Faith does not dismiss doubt. Faith conquers doubt. It means you will go full steam ahead, despite your doubts. Don't let doubt stop you from pursuing what you must.

Use the words, "I've decided to." This is empowering and helps slay doubt.

- I've decided to trust my voice.
- I've decided to I'm going to be in a happy, healthy relationship
- I've decided to develop qualities to attract my ideal mate.
- I've decided to stop settling for less.
- I've decided to raise the bar.
- I've decided to have more love in my life.
- I've decided I'm going to have more money in my life.
- I've decided to trust my knowledge, skills and abilities.
- I've decided to be more confident and courageous.
- I've decided to be strong.
- I've decided to do it now.

Repeat those words or substitute your own. Define what it is that you decided to pursue. Well-defined goals are like magnets. The better you chisel them, the stronger the pull. When you decide, you put focus on your desire and it must come despite any doubts. What you focus on, you feel. What you radiate outward in your thoughts, words and feelings, you attract into your life.

Look, the hero is a hero because the hero does it anyway. Even though the hero is terrified and risking it all, he goes anyway. Be the hero in your own life, in your own story.

Faith alone is not enough. Faith without action is meaningless. When you act in the face of doubt, you develop your competency muscle and that leads to more confidence in your abilities. So instead of letting doubt hold you back, allow doubt to catapult you to where you want to go in life. Master doubt now so that it does not enslave you later.

And there you have it. If you want to go deeper with me on this subject, sign up for my academy training here: http://bit.ly/MyFreeBonus

Chapter 14: The Postage Stamp & How to Be Truly Happy & Fulfilled

Consider the postage stamp. You might think that you are the only happy camper when your package arrives, but you would be wrong. The postage stamp is just as happy as you are. The postage stamp did its job. Because it was looking out for you the whole time, it brought you happiness by giving, and in turn, your happiness made the postage stamp happy too. What can you learn about happiness from the postage stamp's example?

What brings true happiness?

One psychologist said that happiness has three components.

- Pleasure
- Engagement
- Meaning

So let's take a look at these three areas.

Many people build their lives around pleasure, but this is the least consequential. Pleasure must not be your main pursuit in life, or you'll find yourself unhappy. But in moderation, pleasure is something to be enjoyed and savored.

When you are fully engaged in your work and family, you can feel alive and accomplish many things, but when you add meaning to your pursuit of happiness, that is working toward a larger end or goal that is greater than self, then you've hit the trifecta.

I personally follow the nine beatitudes for optimal happiness:

Love moves others to love you in return.
Joy gives you the strength to cope with challenges.
Peace helps you to keep your relationships free of strife.
Patience enables you to stay happy even when you are under trial.
Kindness draws others to you.

Goodness on your part makes others respond when you need help.

Faith will assure you of God's loving direction.

Mildness will bring you calmness of heart, mind, and body.

Self-control means that your mistakes will be fewer.

I also like what author Brendon Burchard says, "Happiness comes from an orientation towards the world in which we look at the past, the present, and the future in specific ways.

He explains that we need to find a way to be at peace with the past. When we do so, we will be freer to accept our present. When we accept our present we can learn to anticipate the excitement of the future.

I'm personally excited about moving to Japan in the near future. What are you excited about? What can you get excited about?

Brendon says. "If you can't find anything to be excited about tomorrow, that has nothing to do with the reality of tomorrow; it has to do with your mindset." Change your mindset and your whole world will change with it.

As a recap:

- Be accepting and at peace with the past.
- Be present and engaged here in the present.
- Be excited. Anticipate something for the future.

If you want true fulfillment in life, you have to kill your comfort zone.

Think of your comfort zone as a self-imposed prison you've put yourself in. It consists of limiting thoughts and ideas about who you are and what you are capable of becoming. Perhaps you learned these limitations while you were young and they are still holding you hostage.

In order to live the life you want, you have to believe you are worth it and then take precise steps to make it happen. It all starts with killing your comfort zone, all those limiting beliefs.

It's time for a prison break!

You can make this shift by exchanging those negative thoughts with positive ones and doing something every day that gets you out of your comfort zone.

Remember the words of Eleanor Roosevelt, "You must do one thing every day that scares you." I agree. Now is the time to take your first scary step toward becoming the person you were meant to be.

And there you have it. If you want to go deeper with me on this subject, sign up for my academy training here: http://bit.ly/MyFreeBonus

Chapter 15: The Postage Stamp & How to Defeat Depression & Anxiety

Consider the postage stamp. It always keeps its cool. It knows it will reach its destination, it may get depressed along the way, but it always bounces back. The postage stamp also uses its anxiety as a tool. Yes, it's anxious because it wants to serve you and bring you happiness as soon as possible, but that never stops it from bringing you its A-game.

According to the World Health Organization 350 million people worldwide suffer from depression. It is a leading cause of disability.

So what causes it?

Many things, but they usually have one thing in common.

- Loss of a loved one
- Loss of a job
- Loss of a home
- Loss of your health
- Loss of a relationship
- Loss of something we think might happen

You can't always control your circumstances, and bad things will affect you at times, but you can develop a practical strategy or framework so that negative feelings do not dominate your life.

First and foremost, seek medical attention. Clinical depression is not momentary sadness but a persistent feeling of despair triggered by a chemical imbalance in your brain. It takes real strength to ask for help. In addition, you may also benefit by confiding your feelings to a close friend. You may be surprised at how relieved you will feel afterwards.

What helped me to overcome depression after suffering the loss of my mother was getting back into a spiritual routine, daily exercise and changing the food I ate. When I spent time comforting others with soothing words from the Bible, I felt I was being healed as well. And when I exercised I felt a certain euphoria that helps me tackle the challenges that we all face on a daily basis. And when I chose better food to eat, I regained energy and strength that allowed me to go on.

Another tool that helped me was reading the book, The Depression Cure by Dr. Stephen Ilardi, which I spoke about earlier, but I'll recap again.

- Consider taking a daily fish oil supplement.
- Be active. Try not to ruminate over negative things. Get outside and move your body and don't forget to connect with others.
- Exercise. This helps improve your physical and mental health.
- Get in the sun. Sunlight stimulates the brains production of serotonin. Serotonin affects your mood and behavior.
- Connect. We need other people. So connect with

someone. Isolation only exacerbates the problem. A great book that I just read covers this in depth, it's called, The Power of the Other, by Dr. Henry Cloud.
- Sleep. Lack of sleep and depression go hand in hand. They are BFFs.

At the outset, I spoke about loss and how it is a common thread for those that are depressed. Let me segway into a close cousin of depression, anxiety.

According to Dr. Ravi Shah, as quoted in Success Magazine, "Anxiety is a natural and healthy feeling all humans experience. It becomes problematic either when the worry is disproportionate to the issue at hand or when it interferes with daily life." He continues, "If worry is holding you back and you get paralyzed by fear –that's when it's a problem."

But there is good news.

Dr. Shah concludes by saying, "Of all the problems in mental health to have, anxiety is in a way a good one because it is very treatable."

Here's another take on it from Brendon. He says, "Anxiety is a sign to pay attention and bring your A-game. You can turn it into drama, a false cataclysmic feeling, or you can use it as a performance enhancement tool."

Brendon lists three primary sources of anxiety and what to do about it:

1. *Fear of loss.* Too often we worry that we could lose respect or love if we fail at something. But most often these are unfounded concerns or faulty assumptions driven by a fearful, *tired* or undirected mind. The next time you feel anxiety, take a few deep breathes and ask, "Can I use this energy to prepare to gain

something versus sit here and fear losing something? What action could I take to ready myself and minimize the chances things won't go well?" Then brainstorm actions you can take to move forward. Sometimes the easiest way to wipe out anxiety is to get a little momentum.

2. *Fear of hardship.* A lot of anxiety comes from feeling like we aren't strong or capable enough to handle a difficult situation. But we have to question this assumption as well. Often, we've been through a lot worse and survived. And now we can use the anxiety to take a step back and better prepare for this upcoming challenge. We can turn anxiety into a strength, into a preparation weapon. No matter what is coming up, you can handle it if you prepare, ask for help, and open yourself to learning and being courageous in tough situations. The tools to manage the difficulties of life are within.

3. *Fear of disappointment.* Often anxiety comes from the fear that we'll feel sad

or experience negative feelings if things don't turn out well. But perhaps it's time to focus on the journey rather than the destination. Just focus on bringing your best to the situation at hand, and remember that everything will turn out well as long as you're open to learning and asking for help along the way. All will be well as long as you stay in motion toward your dreams.

So, how have you been using anxiety? *As a performance enhancement tool or an excuse to stop?*

Burchard says, "The world's highest performers use it as a tool. They get an edge from it and they, "Ok, I'm nervous but that tells me I'm in the game. I better pay attention."

And they also develop plans to develop themselves, to strengthen themselves in all their areas:

- Emotionally
- Socially
- Financially
- Physically

- Spiritually

So that those anxieties start to diminish as they become more.

But honestly, we are always going to have anxiety. So you need to trust yourself to figure it out. The best way to do that is to ask, "Where's this coming from?"

"Sometimes, the best way to overcome anxiety is to re-charge or re-aim your focus towards the things that you do want," Brendon insists.

And there you have it. If you want to go deeper with me on this subject, sign up for my academy training here: http://bit.ly/MyFreeBonus

Chapter 16: The Postage Stamp & How to Stay Focused

Consider the postage stamp. The postage stamp knows it has only one job to do and it does it well. It does not try to accomplish any other goal except for the one that was assigned to it. It has laser focus. It will not sleep until it finishes its one job. What about you?

It has been said that in life, you get what you focus on. This rule applies to every endeavor in your life whether it's starting a business, getting a raise, or wanting to get married, where your attention goes, energy flows. What you focus on expands.

Why is this important?

Because ultimately, your focus drives everything you do. It drives your thoughts, which leads to your feelings and emotions which determine how you will live your life.

If you focus on negative things, you are unwittingly inviting negativity into your life. You will find that when you focus on the negative things in your life, more negative things will occur so you can focus on them. That's how it works. You get in life what you focus on. If you focus on pain, more painful things will happen so you can continue to focus on it.

But, thank goodness, the opposite is also true. If you focus on the positive things in life, you will find more positive things happening to you.

So below are three practical things you can do to focus on what you really want out of life and how to get what you want in the next 100 days.

One of my favorite motivational speakers was the late Zig Ziglar. When it came to the topic of goals, he flat out sold you on the concept. He asked are you a "meaningful specific" or a "wandering generality?" In other words, do you have a definite, specific clear plan of action for your life and career or are you just along for the ride, wandering through life?

The next thing Zig advised was to ink your goal with pen and paper. A goal that is not written is just a dream – one you will never attain.

Did you know that the act of writing actually sharpens your thinking and stimulates your creativity? When you write, you can only focus on one thing at a time. This forces you to spend that time on your goal. Remember, whatever you focus on you feel and what you feel you act on. Below are three creative ways to get your life back on track and finally attain what you really want out of life.

1. I want you to go to the store and buy three boards. Two of the boards will be large and the other medium-sized. Place one board in your office, one in your home and the medium-sized one in your car – the three places where you spend the most time. On these boards, I want you to cut out pictures that represent the three most important goals you want to accomplish this year.

Every morning when you wake up, you will see a visual picture of the goals you wish to accomplish. When you drive to work, you will see the same three pictures and when you get to work you will see the same three pictures again. All this reinforcement will help your mind find ways to make what you want become a reality.

New York Times Best-Selling Author Brendon Burchard says, "Major challenges, major frustrations and major problems in our lives, demand multiple areas of attack. It's like when you go to war, you send in the planes, the ground troops and people from the flank and the front. You go at it from all sides trying to win."

So if you have a major challenge, problem or struggle in your life, or some goal you desperately want to reach, you need to attack from all sides.

2. Use your phone to alert you of goals – at least 3 times a day. A lot of people under utilize this great feature on their iPhones. Right now, I want you to your "Clock" then hit "Alarm" then add your alarm time. Then under "Label" write out your goal – the

same one you have a picture of on your board. Press "Save". Repeat this step three times for each of your goals. So from now on, every day at that time, you'll be reminded to accomplish your goals. This is how you attack from all sides. You have the vision board, you have the alarm and now let's move on to tip number three. This will keep you focused on what you want to accomplish.

3. The purpose of any goal I believe is to create freedom in some area of your life. Who of us wouldn't love to pursue everything we want with no restraints. But sadly, most of us are constrained by our jobs, our finances or both. Entrepreneur on Fire host John Lee Dumas has come up with a way to accomplish everything you want in the next 100 days with his Freedom Journal. The journal will guide you over the next 100 days to set a plan of action, to focus, to

review, accomplish, identify and execute your goals. This is a built-in accountability partner. Most entrepreneurs don't succeed because they are not accountable to anyone. This journal is your accountability buddy. So stop procrastinating and start living the life you were meant to live.

And there you have it. If you want to go deeper with me on this subject, sign up for my academy training here: http://bit.ly/MyFreeBonus

Chapter 17: The Postage Stamp & How to Have More Confidence

Consider the postage stamp. In order to get from where you are to where you want to be, you have to know two things – where you are and where you want to go. If you don't like where you are now and you want to get to a different place in your life, you need to have one very crucial thing –confidence. The postage stamp has great confidence because it takes massive action to get to you.

Scientists used to believe that humans responded to information flowing into the brain from the outside world. But today, they're learning more and more that we respond to what the brain expects to happen next.

Neuropsychologists call it the expectancy theory. Basically, through a lifetime's worth of events, our brains actually learn what to expect next – even if it does not happen. And because our brain expects something will happen a certain way, we often achieve exactly what we anticipate.

Do you see the dilemma?

If you don't expect much to happen in your life, then, most likely it won't. But if you do expect something great to occur, it most likely will. The difference is that you have to believe it will happen for you. But how do you get that belief?

Simply put, you need to build your confidence.

Confidence is another way of saying you need to believe in yourself. Believing in yourself is a choice. It's an attitude you develop over time. All you have to do is choose to believe that you can do anything that you set your mind to – anything at all – because, in fact, you can.

The more bold and courageous you are, the bolder and more courageous you'll be in the future. The more confident you are today, the more confident you'll be in the future. The opposite is also true, if you choose weakness today, you're more likely to choose weakness tomorrow.

Listed below are five more tips taken from my mentor, Brendon, on what it takes to have more confidence.

To have confidence:

1. Decide to have it. Make it an intention. You don't need to achieve anything more, you simply need to decide to feel and generate confidence

on a more consistent and conscious basis.

2. Live with integrity for who you are and what you believe. When you are being fully alive and authentic and true to yourself, you feel confident.

3. Get more competent. Go gather more knowledge, skill, and abilities in the areas that you are passionate about and need to perform well in. More competence = more confidence.

4. Get momentum. Take more action. Life isn't about perfection it's about progress. The more action you take the more progress you'll sense and the more confident you'll feel that you are on path.

5. Surround yourself with positive, supportive people. If you don't have a supportive community, go create one. No excuses. A positive peer set will help you feel more confident

Martin Luther King said, "Faith is taking the first step even when you don't see the staircase." After you take that first step toward confidence and away from fear, you will see other opportunities opening up for you. The universe will see your intention and help you find a way to make it happen. But you first have to believe it can happen for you.

And there you have it. If you want to go deeper with me on this subject, sign up for my academy training here: http://bit.ly/MyFreeBonus

Chapter 18: The Postage Stamp & How to Handle Money

Consider the postage stamp. It never exceeds its capacity. It never tries to do more than it can do. It does not borrow or ask for help from other stamps. It lives within its means, works hard and gets the job done. It never sticks to what it cannot chew. What about you?

New York Times Best-Selling Author Dave Ramsey once said, "I am positive that personal finance is 80 percent behavior and only 20 percent head knowledge." Ramsey believes it our behaviors around money that makes us continually fall into debt and live a life of struggle.

But, just like with anything, if you want to change your behavior with money, you have to do just that, change. But change is painful, right? Very few people view change in a positive light. Unfortunately, most people won't change until the pain of where they are exceeds the pain of change. That's why, according to CNN Money, a whopping 76 percent of Americans live from paycheck to paycheck.

The best way to handle money is to be willing to delay pleasure. If you are willing, Ramsey says in his book, The Total Money Makeover, "If you live like no one else, later you can live like no one else." This means that if you make the sacrifices now that most people aren't willing to make, later on you will be able to live as other people never will. But you must delay your need to spend money now. You need to stop giving into instant gratification.

Another good book to help with finances is by Rachel Cruze, she is the daughter of Dave Ramsey. She wrote, Love Your Life, Not Theirs – 7 Money Habits for Living the Life You Want. She believes in G.S.S. which stands for giving, saving and then spending your money. I like that principle because when you focus on giving, more will be given to you to give to others.

Also make sure you are automatically investing your money. When get a check from your employer, have some of the funds automatically go into your savings account or investment account. This way you won't forget and you won't spend the money unnecessarily. Automatically investing means your money will be earning money for you and working for you. Check out the book: The Automatic Millionaire by David Bach.

You need to visualize your life without debt, what would your life be like? But many times even this visualization is difficult. Just as slaves born into slavery can't visualize freedom, people the world over, can't visualize a life with no debt. But it is possible!

I highly recommend the book, _**The Total Money Makeover by Dave Ramsey**_, not only does he list practical steps to get out of debt, he interviews dozens of couples that tell exactly how they got out of debt using his system. If they can do it, you can do it too.

And there you have it. If you want to go deeper with me on this subject, sign up for my academy training here: http://bit.ly/MyFreeBonus

Chapter 19: The Postage Stamp & How to be the Most Memorable Person in the Room or 7 Scientific Steps to Increase Your Influence

Consider the postage stamp. The postage is always confident and poised. It knows its self-worth. It leaves an immediate impression on anything that it is stuck to. Without it, the letter or package will never arrive at its destination. It has the ultimate influence.

Udemy.com instructor Vanessa Van Edwards, is a behavioral investigator.

Her mission in life is to help individuals become the most memorable person in the room.

Van Edwards refers to herself as a recovering boring person who was hopelessly bland. So she turned to science to overcome her dilemma. By using current research from academic institutions and research organizations around the world, she says, she can share the latest in people science in an actionable, applicable and unboring way.

She has a number of classes on Udemy.com specifically geared to helping entrepreneurs maximize their potential. If you take her free Udemy course of the same name, which I highly recommend, this is what you'll learn:

1. Connect with people emotionally.

Van Edwards says she has discovered that if you want to intrigue and influence people, you have to get their dopamine pumping. She has based her research on the findings of <u>molecular biologist John Medina</u>.

Dopamine stimulates that pleasure-reward area in the brain that makes people feel all warm and fuzzy. She says you need to be relentless about stimulating that part of the brain if you want to influence someone.

A great way to do that is by having excellent conversation starters handy. Here are two that Van Edwards always uses: "What was the best part of your day and what was the worst part of your day?" and "What personal passion project are you currently working on right now?"

2. Be emotionally curious.

When you make others feel important, your influence goes a long way. Everyone wants to be liked, loved and accepted. When you fulfill that need for others, you are perceived as being influential.

Become genuinely interested in other people. A great way to do this is to ask them open-ended questions. Get people talking about themselves and that will help you build rapport. According to postdoctoral scholar Diana Tamir, a person disclosing information about himself or herself will be intrinsically rewarding.

3. Use high-powered body language.

Researchers at Harvard Business School conducted a study exploring if an individual's body language could affect other people's opinions of that person, as Van Edwards explains in her Udemy.com class. It turns out that that is what the research found.

Low-powered body language is normally contracted, with the shoulders rolled and the head down or bowed.

High-powered or confident body language is expansive. The head is held high, the arms are loose, the shoulders are set back and the chest is out. When you manifest powerful body language, you are seen as more influential. Confident body language not only affects the way others see you but also the way you see yourself.

4. Tell a story.

People's brains are almost hard-wired for stories. When people hear stories, they can feel as if they are right there with the other person. It's like the listener is experiencing the story along with the narrator.

Do you see the potential of how influential storytelling could make you? When someone tells a story, the brain of the other person may be in sync with the storyteller. If you can stimulate the other person's brain with a story, you can, in effect, get that person on your side.

Van Edwards suggests creating a story toolbox. This toolbox should consist of relevant and thought-provoking stories that you can tell at any time when you're with people. Then after you tell the story, follow it up with some interesting questions.

She likes to ask, "What was your most challenging moment and how did you overcome it?" and "When did a person, situation or moment turn out differently than you expected?

5. Be vulnerable.

Being open about your emotions increases your likeability and influence. People will perceive you as being real when you admit to weaknesses or flaws.

Some people are fearful because of something called the spotlight effect, thinking that others are paying more attention to them than they truly are, according to *Psychology Today*.

But the opposite is true. People are able to better relate to you when you open up. Even though you are the center of your world, you're not the center of everyone else's. Van Edwards suggests sharing a vulnerable story from your story toolbox. By doing this, you not only tell a great story but you also are being vulnerable, so it increases your influence in two ways.

6. Ask a favor.

According to Van Edwards' Udemy.com class, whenever a person asks someone else for a favor, he or she is perceived more positively.

It turns out that asking for help is one of the best things you could do to be perceived as an influential person. This is known as the <u>Benjamin Franklin effect.</u> So freely ask for help in the form of advice, other people's opinions and their guidance.

7. Become charismatic.

Who is the most charismatic person you know? Why did you pick that person? Most likely you chose that individual because of the way that person makes you feel.

According to research performed at the <u>MIT Media Lab</u>, most people don't remember what an individual looks like or what he or she might have said. They remember how the individual made them feel.

Charismatic people make others feel good. Van Edwards provides three nonverbal ways for a person to increase his or her charisma quotient. When talking to someone, tilt your head, align your torso with that person's and point your toes toward the person, she says.

And there you have it. If you want to go deeper with me on this subject, sign up for my academy training here: http://bit.ly/MyFreeBonus

Chapter 20: The Postage Stamp & How to Raise Your Standards in Every Area of Your Life

Consider the postage stamp. When it comes to standards, the postage stamp can go no higher. Whatever the letter or

package costs, the postage stamp is willing to pay the price. It does not ask for a discount or to be sent free. It pays what is asked of it. Its standards are among the highest in the world. What about you?

What is the difference between something you should do and something you absolutely must do?

Motivational speaker Jim Rohn said, "The things easy to do are also easy not to do." In other words, the things you should do are things that are easy not to do and so you don't do them. Some of these things are:

I should eat healthier.

I should exercise more.

I should treat my spouse with respect.

But when you absolutely must do something, as if your life depended on it, there is a shift and change in you. If eating healthier meant you would live or die, then you most likely would do it. The same with exercise and treating your spouse with respect, if your life depended on it, you would make the necessary changes.

When you raise your standards and turn "should" into "must," you are making an inner shift to take control over the quality of your life. Any area in which you are not getting what you want is because you haven't **raised your standards**.

According to Tony Robbins, "Most people, if they look at how they are living their lives today, will find that their identity is based on a set of standards and a set of beliefs they created 10, 20, 30 or more years ago. In fact, many of us made decisions when we were kids about what to believe, what we are capable, and who we are as a person, and that became the glass ceiling that controls us. But are you the same person you were back then? Are you the same person you were even a year ago?"

I'm just going to say it, you have to demand excellence from yourself. Don't be mediocre. Be world-class. Don't settle for status-quo, be relentless.

Pursue excellence. "People are rewarded in public for what they've practiced for years in private," said Tony Robbins. Never ever give up. Raise your standards.

Best-selling Author Brendon Burchard says if you raise your standards in these five areas, your life will dramatically improve:

1. Health. Have you ever said, "This is going to be the year I get in the best health of my life"? If not, this is the year to do it. Improve your health and becoming happier and more energized and effective happens almost automatically. Raise your standards on how much sleep you get and how well you eat and take care of your body.

2. Focus. Distraction is stealing your life. Get more focused on what you desire in this hour, this day, this life. Bring your awareness to this moment and what you want to be doing and experiencing now. That will help you be more conscious and more easily spot distractions.

3. Boldness. Where you are in life right now is a direct reflection of how bold you've been up to this point. How boldly do you share yourself, your ideas, your needs and dreams with the world? How courageous have you been to fight after you've fallen down. Demand of yourself to be more bold and you'll feel more confident and influential over time.

4. Joy. Do you expect that you're going to have fun today and in life? Better yet, do you demand of yourself to be the person who brings the joy, who has fun and helps others have fun no matter what? Joy is a choice not a happenstance blessing. Bring the joy.

5. Kindness. People are so driven and distracted that they've often lost the awareness to be kind to others. They might call themselves compassionate, but they are not kind. Kindness is compassion activated - you actually show you care through your actions. Raising your standard here will help you reach higher levels of happiness, service, and humanity.

And there you have it. If you want to go deeper with me on this subject, sign up for my academy training here: http://bit.ly/MyFreeBonus

Chapter 21: The Postage Stamp & How to Create Side-Hustle Income Teaching What You Already Know

Consider the postage stamp. The postage stamp is not stingy. It freely shares. When it is placed on a mail piece, it can't wait to share the contents inside with the recipient. It is always looking for an opportunity to give. It teaches by example. What can you teach that is already intrinsically inside of you?

What if you were given the opportunity to get paid for sharing with other people information you already?

Now, perhaps unlike at any other time in history, if you possess knowledge that other people would be willing to pay for, you can start making money, with little or no startup costs.

Teaching online grants you the freedom to still work a day job yet generate side-hustle income. In fact, today, it's a real possibility to even make just as much money while you're asleep as when you're awake, thanks to the power of the Internet.

You have the opportunity to teach and share what you're most passionate about to large audiences. Would you like to share what you love and be paid for doing so? One vehicle for doing so is Udemy.com, which describes itself as an "online learning marketplace" with a mission "to help anyone learn anything."

"The world is changing so quickly and gotten more complex, especially because of technology that people need to constantly learn new things," Udemy's CEO, Dennis Yang told me in an interview.

"There's been a cultural shift towards sharing and just like Netflix, people want to be able control their own media," Yang adds. "Because of mobile technology, people want access to learning when they want it and where they want it."

A new instructor, he says "has the ability to impact many students' lives and students have access to experts, right at their fingertips," he says.

Before you cast your hat in the online teaching ring, do these three things first:

1. Claim a topic.

What area do you find fascinating? In everyday conversation, what do you talk about the most? This could be an indication of what you could teach others.

What questions are people always asking you to help them with? If individuals are always approaching you for advice, perhaps within that there's something you can teach.

What genre of books do you tend to read? Answering this might point to a subject area you might teach.

2. Solve a problem.

To teach what you already know -- or what you are willing to learn -- you require students. And to find them, you must know their needs and how to best serve them.

Asking questions is the best way to familiarize yourself with the needs of prospective students.

You might ask, for example, some of these questions:

What are three areas in which you're having problems at work or in life?

What are three things you really want to accomplish this year?

What frustrates you the most about your job?

What have you done to try to improve your situation? What has worked the best (or the least)?

3. Define an objective.

Remember, you want to deliver only high-quality information. To so, you must know your audience and cater to their needs. A good question to ask yourself is "Who are the people who will participate in my course and what will they be hoping to learn?"

Focus on students at a specific skill level: beginners, intermediate or advanced learners. This will not only help you target the right audience but will also ensure that your course offers the type of information that your students are seeking.

Nick Walter, who made $60,000 in 30 days by promoting his Udemy.com class on Kickstarter.com, has shared with me details of his teaching experiences. He didn't even have a regular job at the time. That just goes to show you the power of teaching what you know.

How much extra money would you like to make next year?

Do you have that number in your head? Consider how easy it can be earn extra cash just by teaching what you already know.

By the end of this year, you'll end up somewhere. Do you want to end up somewhere well-designed or undesigned?

The choice is yours.

And there you have it. If you want to go deeper with me on this subject, sign up for my academy training here: http://bit.ly/MyFreeBonus

Chapter 22: The Postage Stamp & How to Say I'm Sorry and Express Forgiveness

Consider the postage stamp. The postage stamp feels sorrow and pain when it does not reach its destination on time and it is sorry for the delay. When the letter or package finally arrives it in effect is saying, "I am sorry for the delay, please forgive me."

Why is it so hard for some people to apologize?

The magazine, The Watchtower states, "One reason why a person hesitates to apologize may be the fear of rejection. Troubled by the thought of being given the cold shoulder, he may not express how he really feels. While the person who was hurt might totally avoid the offender, making reconciliation very difficult.

"A lack of concern for other people's feelings may be another reason why some hesitate to apologize. They may reason, 'Apologizing will not undo the blunder I have already made.' Still others hesitate to say that they are sorry because of the possible consequences. They wonder, 'Will I be held responsible and be asked to make compensation?' However, the biggest hurdle to admitting a mistake is pride. A person who is too proud to say "I am sorry" may in essence conclude, 'I don't want to lose face by admitting my blunder. That would weaken my position.'"

For whatever reason, many find words of apology hard to utter. But is it really necessary to apologize? What are the benefits of apologizing?"

"Apologies are powerful. They resolve conflicts without violence, repair schisms between nations, allow governments to acknowledge the suffering of their citizens, and restore equilibrium to personal relationships." So wrote Deborah Tannen, a best-selling author and sociolinguist at Georgetown University in Washington, D.C.

It is important to be sincere when extending an apology. If we are sincere, our apology will include an admission of any wrong, a seeking of forgiveness, and an effort to undo damage to the extent possible.

Forgiveness is the act of pardoning an offender; ceasing to feel resentment toward him because of his offense and giving up all claim to recompense. Forgiveness is about empowering yourself. Best-selling author Brendon Burchard says, "Forgiving is so simple. It literally is a decision. No justification or cause has to happen, and forgiving does not have to do anything with accepting the other person's behavior, approving of it, justifying it, rationalizing it or understanding it."

Medical research has shown that when we hold onto resentment and fail to apologize and forgive, we are only making ourselves sick, literally. Such negative emotions can rob us of happiness, restrict our life, and make us miserable. They can also pose a serious health risk. A report in the *Journal of the American College of Cardiology,* by Dr. Yoichi Chida and Professor of Psychology Andrew Steptoe, concluded: "The current findings suggest a harmful association between anger and hostility and CHD [coronary heart disease]."

When we forgive others we are in essence healing ourselves.

In addition, according to a publication of the Mayo Clinic, it say, "If you don't practice forgiveness, you might be the one who pay most dearly." Forgiveness, the article explains, can result in "healthier relationships, greater spiritual and psychological well-being, less anxiety, stress, hostility, lower blood pressure, fewer symptoms of depression and lower risk of alcohol and substance abuse."

So make the decision today that you will let go of whatever is hurting you. You are in the driver's seat. You have the power to stop the pain that you are experiencing.

And there you have it. If you want to go deeper with me on this subject, sign up for my academy training her: http://bit.ly/MyFreeBonus

Chapter 23: The Postage Stamp & How to Create Bulletproof Habits

Consider the postage stamp. The postage stamp is the king or if you will, queen of bulletproof habits. The postage stamp has only one goal. It will not deviate from that goal. It has established a habit of only sticking to that goal. That habit will never be broken. The postage stamp always stays the course.

In 2008, after my mom died of colon and liver cancer, a few years later, I developed the habit of getting up at 4 a.m. and going to the gym. That habit has helped and sustained me all these years. I knew I had to do something to get my mind out of the loop of negativity. I knew I had to physically move my body because where your focus goes, energy flows.

With that said, I started researching other high achievers and came across Brendon Burchard. I quote him a lot in this book as you know. That's because what he says really resonates with me and has helped me become the person I am today. I curate only the best. Brendon has been studying high achievers for over 20 years and the biggest secret he has learned when it comes to habits is "trigger moments."

In essence, trigger moments are cues that remind you to activate your intentions or habits.

Burchard says, "It's one thing to have the intention to be more kind, patient and loving with people; it's quite another to set a reminder on your phone that triggers you into being that kind of person. It's one thing to want to eat healthier but another to setup a mental trigger that says, "Every time I drop off my kids at school, I immediately go to the gym or drive to the grocery store and buy fresh produce." A trigger is a "when this thing happens, then I do or think that."

In order to set up bullet-proof habits, using trigger moments is a must.

Burchard goes on to say, "For example, if you want to become more present and calm throughout the day, set up three phone alarms to go off throughout the day with a label that says, "Close your eyes, take ten deep breaths in, and remind yourself to be calm." These reminders will trigger you to enact the new behavior.

"One of his favorite triggers to set up are **"doorframe triggers."** Here's how it works: When you walk into a room you have a psychological trigger go off in your mind that you've associated with that doorframe. So, for example, when you walk into the office in the morning, have three words go through your mind about how you want to interact with other people. Set up this same kind of trigger for when you walk into meetings, conference rooms, and even when you walk into your house.

"Whatever you want to achieve in your life - better health, more energy, more clarity - set a trigger.

"If you set up more triggers reminding yourself to stick to your habits and intentions, everything in your life will change. You will feel more energized, engaged and on track," according to Burchard.

I personally use three things that help me maintain and sustain my habits. I use visual boards. I have cut out the same pictures and put them on my board in my office and at my house. Every morning when I wake up, I see the boards and when I come to work, I see the exact same thing. All this reinforcement helps my mind find ways to make what I want become a reality.

I also use my iPhone to create alerts to help reinforce what I see on the boards. A lot of people under utilize this great feature on their iPhones. Right now, I want you to your "Clock" then hit "Alarm" then add your alarm time. Then under "Label" write out your goal – the same one you have a picture of on your board. Press "Save". Repeat this step three times for each of your goals. So from now on, every day at that time, you'll be reminded to accomplish your goals. This is how you attack from all sides. You have the vision board, you have the alarm and now let's move on to tip number three.

My all-time favorite bullet-proof habit device is the pen and paper. When we track what we do, things get done. As an example, I started using the Fitbit. This device tracks how many steps you take in a day. Before I had this device, I never walked 10,000 steps, but now that I track it, I make sure I do it every day. The same is true with any habit you form. When you write it down and track it, you will see the needle move, your results will encourage you to continue going. This helps to build momentum and you will become unstoppable.

And there you have it. If you want to go deeper with me on this subject, sign up for my academy training here: http://bit.ly/MyFreeBonus

Chapter 24: The Postage Stamp & How to Learn Faster

Consider the postage stamp. If ever the postage stamp can get to you, the recipient faster, it does all it can. When it is sent through mail processing machinery, it is hoping that it will be picked first and put into the driver's vehicle. It wants to reach its destination as quickly as possible. Speed and accuracy are what it strives for.

Your brain is the hardware of your soul. It is the hardware of your very essence as a human being. So the only way to learn faster, is to learn to harness your brain power.

One way to help your brain according to brain fitness studies is to make it a practice to remember events, things and people's name. Memory activities engage the brain on all levels and it will help you to learn faster and retain what you learn.

The next thing you can do to learn faster is by doing something new over and over again until it sticks. Through repetition, your brain forms new pathways that will help you do this new thing better and faster.

Moving on, the next thing you can do to learn faster may sound counterproductive, but it actually works. You need to learn a new language. I have been learning Portuguese for the past 10 years and it is finally sinking in. In the beginning I had major difficulties, only because I did not start speaking right away, because of my own fears, but when I started speaking the language, things really took off and I began to learn faster. In addition, learning a new language exposes your brain to a new culture and people and by learning their customs, it can help make you a more tolerant and understanding person, not to mention, it exposes your brain to different way of thinking which leads to a different way of expressing yourself, which can help you to learn even faster.

The next thing you need to do is work your body. Yes, you need to get out and exercise. I exercise five days a week and I feel fantastic and amazing each and every day. Even briefly exercising for 20 minutes facilitates information processing and memory functions. But it's not just that–exercise actually helps your brain create those new neural connections faster. You will learn faster, your alertness level will increase, and you get all that by moving your body.

Bonding with loved ones is the next thing you need to do if you want to learn faster. If you want optimal cognitive abilities, then you've got to have meaningful relationships in your life. Talking with others and engaging with your loved ones helps you think more clearly, and it can also lift your mood, which helps you learn faster because you are in a positive mood.

Dr. Stephen Illardi says in his book, The Depression Cure, "We are born to connect. It is etched in our DNA. We need other people. When we are deprived of social contact for just a few days, our stress hormones escalate, our mood and energy plummet and other key biological processes quickly begin to decline. Isolation exacerbates depression. Social withdrawal amplifies depression. Conversely, anything that enhances social connectedness helps us fight depression."

And lastly, you need to feed your brain proper nutrition in order for it to function properly. Foods like fish, fruits, and vegetables help your brain perform optimally. When your brain is hitting on all cylinders, you can't help but to learn faster.

And there you have it. If you want to go deeper with me on this subject, sign up for my academy training here: http://bit.ly/MyFreeBonus

Chapter 25: The Postage Stamp & How to Expect More and Get More

Consider the postage stamp. The postage stamp expects to get where it is going. It does not doubt. It does not fear. It knows where it is going and it will always get there. It expects to arrive and put a smile on your face. It always gets what it expects.

You've heard the adage, "A mind is a terrible thing to waste." It is so very true. In fact the mind is so powerful, that neuropsychologists now believe that we get in life what the brain expects to happen to us next. In other words, they say we spend our whole life becoming conditioned. Through a lifetime's worth of events, our brain actually learns what to expect next. And because we expect it, we often get it. Do you realize how powerful that is?

If you expect more out of your life, you will get it. But the opposite is also true, if you don't expect much, you will hit that target every time. The power is literally in your head.

So if financial freedom is something you want, you have to believe you are capable of making it happen. Believing in yourself is a choice. It's an attitude you develop over time. It is up to you to choose to be a better, more successful person.

I personally love our brains. Two main factors seem responsible for how our brain develops throughout our lifetime – what we allow to enter it through our senses and what we choose to think about. The brain therefore is deeply affected by our experiences and our thinking.

So surround yourself with positive people and think about positive things. Believe that you will get that which you deeply desire. You have to train your brain to expect greatness in the future. Only then will you attain it.

Over time, what we expect to happen to us often does. So expect good things from yourself, from others, and from the world.

And there you have it. If you want to go deeper with me on this subject, sign up for my academy training here: http://bit.ly/MyFreeBonus

Chapter 26: The Postage Stamp & How to Improve Your Self-Esteem and Self-Image

Consider the postage stamp. The postage stamp knows its worth. It knows that it is one-of-a-kind. When it is placed on your mail piece, it knows that it see you very soon. This is the legacy of the postage stamp. Its great grandmothers and grandfathers have all reached their goals. That sense of legacy gives it pride and that pride enables the postage stamp to think highly of itself.

In a talk at TEDx San Francisco, Mel Robbins, self-help author of the book, The 5 Second Rule, mentioned that scientists estimate the probability of your being born at about one in 400 trillion.

Do you know what that means?

It means you are engineered for success and designed to have high levels of self-esteem, self-respect and personal pride. You are extraordinary. There has never been anyone exactly like you in all history of mankind on the earth. You have amazing untapped talents and abilities that, when properly directed and applied, can bring you everything you could ever want or dream of.

In essence, your very existence proves you are a miracle. So start acting like the miracle you are!

In a CD by Earl Nightingale, titled, The Strangest Secret, he says, "You literally become what you think about." So what are you thinking? What are you constantly feeding your mind on? Your mistakes or your accomplishments?

Your thoughts trigger images and pictures and the emotions that go with them. These images then trigger your attitudes and actions. Therefore, if you think about success, you will feel strong and competent, but when you think about your mistakes, you will inevitably feel sad and weak.

We attract into our lives that which we think about. Whatever our dominant thoughts are, that is what will show up for us in our lives. In order to have more self-esteem you need to think the thoughts you would be thinking if you were already achieving your goal.

According to Brian Tracy in his book, Change Your Thinking, Change Your

Life, he says there are three parts to your self-concept and that all three elements make up your personality.

The first part is your self-ideal which is made up of all your hopes, dreams, and ideals. It is the things you most admire in yourself and others. It is the person you would most like to become.

The second part is your self-image. This is the way you see yourself and think about yourself. It's often called your inner mirror. Maxwell Maltz believed that by visualizing and imagining yourself performing at your best in an upcoming situation, you send a message to your subconscious mind which accepts this message as a command and then coordinates your thoughts and actions to fit a pattern consistent with the picture you created of yourself.

The third part of your self-concept is your self-esteem. This is the emotional component of your personality and is the most important factor in determining how you think, feel and behave. Self-esteem is best defined as how much you like yourself. It determines much of what happens to you in life.

Whenever you do or say something that is not in keeping with your ideals or the best in way in which you could act, your self-esteem goes down. On the other hand, every improvement in any part of your personality or performance boots your self-esteem and causes you to like and respect yourself even more. The more you like yourself, the more you will achieve what you want in life because you will believe it is possible. In addition, the more you like yourself, the less you fear failure and the less concerned you are with the opinions of others. The more you like yourself, the more committed you will be to pursuing your goals and raising your standards and the less you will care about what other think or say about you.

Remember to love yourself. You are unique among the seven billion-plus people on this planet. Recognize and honor that uniqueness.

And there you have it. If you want to go deeper with me on this subject, sign up

for my academy training here:
http://bit.ly/MyFreeBonus

Chapter 27: Bonus: The Postage Stamp & Delayed Gratification

Consider the postage stamp. It knows it has a job to do and it does it. It may want to visit a fellow stamp friend in a different state, but it delays that instant gratification and opts to get to its intended destination. It knows that waiting to see his stamp friend is a sign of strength not of weakness.

In the book, *Think and Grow Rich*, author Napoleon Hill states, "Sex desire is the most powerful of human desires. So strong and impelling is the desire for sexual contact that men freely run the risk of life and reputation to indulge it."

Would you not agree?

But Hill goes on to pontificate, "The transmutation of sex energy calls for the exercise of will-power. If it is not transmuted into some creative effort it will find a less worthy outlet." In other words, your burning desire to have sex, that sexual energy, needs to be diverted into something creative. In essence, you must delay physical gratification and use that desire to create your masterpiece. You must learn to transform energy.

How can you do this?

By simply shifting your thoughts. The mind is a creature of habit. It thrives upon the dominating thoughts you feed it. You must control your mind. Think of something yellow. Now think of something blue. You just controlled your mind. That type of control comes from a persistence of habit. When negative emotions such as fear and procrastination start to creep in, use your mind to transform it into a positive, constructive emotion. Remember, positive and negative emotions cannot occupy the mind at the same time.

In Quantum Physics, to bring something into the physical world requires focusing not on what you see, but on what you *want* to see. Einstein said, "Matter is formed out of energy." The very substance of what we see and feel came from someone's thoughts or energy. Ergo, not only do our thoughts impact matter, our thoughts are vibrational energy that manifest in what we see in our lives. If you think of scarcity and lack, that is what will show up in your life, because your thoughts are focused on it. Whatever we focus on expands and every experience we feel with our senses only comes after the decision we've made to see, experience and feel it in that way, physicists say. So what we choose to focus on really does matter.

In the book, ***The Wait,*** which centers on celibacy before marriage, husband and wife team DeVon Franklin and Meagan Good comment that, "Mastering delayed gratification has an impact on every area of life from finances to family relationships."

Franklin admits, "The decision to wait was one of the most difficult ones I've ever made in my life. I asked myself, 'What if what I was doing disqualified me for the full manifestation of the call God has on my life.'" He could not reconcile the idea that at the end of his life, all that God had in store for him could not be bestowed upon him because he chose not to delay gratification. Franklin concludes, "As a man, if you can be disciplined in your sexual life, there's nothing you can't do."

I want you to see the principle here. What if success is in your future, but because you cannot delay gratification, you will not ever see it manifested in your life?

When you are able to control your emotions, then you are powerful. Delaying gratification and transforming that energy into something productive and creative is not weakness, it is strength. In delaying gratification, yes, you are denying your immediate urge, but we are endowed with a beautiful thing called willpower. Once you learn to harness the power of your will, success beckons. When you get in a habit of delaying gratification, it will become easier. Remember, our mind is a creature of habit and it thrives upon the thoughts you feed it. Will it be easy?

No, but it can be done. It must be done if you want something more in your life right now.

Speaking of easy, that's one word, you want to use less of in your vocabulary. Please tell me one thing that is worthwhile that is easy. My point exactly. What trips people up when it comes to easy is that whatever is easy to do is also easy not to do, Jim Rohn said. It's easy to exercise, but do you do it? It's easy to get eight hours of sleep, but do you do it? It's easy to eat healthy, but do you do it? See my point.

"Neglect starts off as an infection," said author Jim Rohn. "But it quickly leads to disease." If you neglect to do wise things with your money, you'll be broke. If you neglect to do wise things with your health, you'll end of sick. If you neglect to do that thing that keeps nagging you, you end of with an unfulfilled life.

According to Rohn, the formula for disaster is, "You should do it, you could do it, but you don't do it." Do not neglect. If you do, you'll be driving what you don't want to drive, working where you don't want to work and living where you don't want to live. When you neglect, you have to put up with your own lack.

If you should be walking around the corner every day for your health and you don't, what is that neglect costing you?

Every day, more and more people are getting sick and having to take medication – all because of neglect. They've neglected to take care of their health and now they are suffering the consequences. Don't neglect. For some it is legitimate, but for others and you know who you are, it's simply neglect. How tall does a tree grow? As tall as it can. Be like the tree. Stop settling for less than the best you can do.

You've spent enough time where you are. Move to a new ZIP Code. How long do you want your child to remain in first grade? Exactly. If you demand it of your kids, you have to demand it for yourself. How long have you been stuck where you are? Time to move on. Grieve the person you were in the past and move on. **In her book, _Stop Saying You're Fine: Discover a More Powerful You,_ Mel Robbins,** developed the five second rule to get herself to take action when she didn't want to. The truth is she says, "If you don't start doing the things you don't feel like doing, you will wake up one year from today and be in exactly the same place." Is that the life you want?

Let me ask you this, "When is a rubber band useful?"

Only when it is stretched.

We are the same way. Too many people settle for mediocre and average. The majority of people underestimate themselves. You aim for what you know you can reach and you hit it every time. Instead, you should aim for that thing just beyond your grasp, and not surprisingly, you will hit it too. Do not take this amazing trip through life and never pay the full fare. For every promise there is a price to pay. Just like a rubber band, in life, stretching is required. It starts from the inside out and it's never easy and people will criticize you, but if you want to grow, you must take a risk. If you've never delayed gratification in any area of your life, you must start now. Because the greatest stretching in life comes when we do things that are not easy and that have never been done by us before. Take your common house plant. If it ceases to grow, it dies. Everything that ceases to struggle, dissipates. If you are not active in your life, whether that involves exercising or doing the thing you know you should do, i.e. writing that book, you will also slowly dissipate and die. Abraham Maslow said, "If you plan on being anything less than you are capable of being, you will probably be unhappy all the days of your life."

When you are hungry, what type of signals does your body send you? Perhaps a headache, you might become irritable or your stomach may growl. If you do not obey the signals your body is giving you, you will continue to experience those symptoms until you give your body the food it needs. What signals does your body give you when you fail to pursue that which you know you should? Before I answer that consider what author *Mel Robbins says in her book, Stop Saying You're Fine: Discover a More Powerful You,* "We all want to become something bigger and more powerful than we are. It's built into our DNA. As long as you're breathing, you will be looking for something more. What you decide to do with that feeling – stuff it or act on it – determines the direction of your life."

Maslow's famous hierarchy of needs states that we as humans are all driven to meet our basic needs, such as food, clothing and shelter. But, when these needs are met, new needs arise. You start to long for something more. This normally translates into an urging for a deeper understanding of your life or some kind of creative outlet. When you do not meet your higher needs, you feel sad, unfulfilled and disillusioned with life. Remember that question about what signals your body gives you when you fail to pursue that thing that you know you should, well, that is the answer. The signals are your own emotions. It is how you feel about life. Are you truly happy in every area of your life? If not, it's because you are not creating in your life. You are not participating in your life. You are taking things easy. You do the same things every day and every week and every month. You are not stretching yourself. You are taking what life is dealing out to you. You are not in control. You feel stuck. If that is true of you, then that's good in one sense. This is your wake-up call. Get unstuck. Commandeer your life.

Simply put, if you want to arrive at a new destination, you have to take a new path. "Do not wait for a change of environment before you act. Cause a change of environment through action," said Wallace Wattles. Have a bias toward action.

And there you have it. If you want to go deeper with me on this subject, sign up for my academy training here: http://bit.ly/MyFreeBonus

Chapter 28 Bonus: The Postage Stamp & The Pendulum Effect

Consider the postage stamp. It knows that if it is to deliver happiness to its recipient, it must risk leaving the comfort of its family. It must leave the book of stamps it comes in, in order to attain its ultimate purpose in life. It's risky, the unknown is scary, but there are no risks without great rewards.

When author of The Compound Effect Darren Hardy started in real estate at age 20, he was a complete novice. So, he compensated: At his first real estate seminar, he bravely asked the lecturer to lunch and asked for the man's best tip on being successful. The lecturer told him to go fail and do it often. Hardy was perplexed.

So, the man picked up his napkin and pulled out a pen. He wrote on the napkin that, "Life, growth, and achievement work like a pendulum. On one side you have failure, rejection, pain and sadness. But on the other side, you have success, victory, joy and happiness."

Guess which side we have control over? Right: the side that comes with pain and failure and rejection. In that area, we control our own future.

Hardy's lunch companion continued: "Over time, most people figure out how to operate in a narrow comfort zone. They only allow the pendulum to swing a small distance into pain and rejection and failure; thus, they only experience the same small degree of joy and success on the other side."

But here's the lesson: The pendulum does not take sides. It is neutral. It swings freely on both sides with the same force with which you attack life. As the person swinging the pendulum, you'll find that it is impossible to experience one side -- success and joy -- without the other side, pain and rejection.

So, once you start to pursue your goals, you need to understand that you cannot have ultimate success without failure, just as you cannot have love without heartache. You receive rewards only when you are willing to take risks.

This may all feel to you like a butterfly in flight: What you pursue eludes you, and that's why you can't "chase" success. It has to find you. That happens when you become a person worthy of success. And that happens only when you swing that pendulum as high as you can on the side of failure and rejection.

You pick yourself up. You learn from the experience, and you move on. That's what successful people do. It's what the postage stamp does.

And there you have it. If you want to go deeper with me on this subject, sign up for my academy training here: http://bit.ly/MyFreeBonus

Chapter 29 Bonus: The Postage Stamp & The Law of Paying Attention

Consider the postage stamp. The postage stamp has sharp, laser focus. It does not get distracted. It has only one goal. It pays attention to what it must accomplish. At the end of its days, it will have engraved on its epitaph: "It secured its success through its ability to stick to one thing."

When I interviewed author Darren Hardy, he said, that the greatest challenge today is controlling our attention. "We are living in an era of epic distraction," he said. "There is so much that begs for our attention. We are forever in reaction mode, whether it be to our inbox or social media accounts. But we must learn to be insanely focused.

"Some say that the problem is an overabundance of information. It's not the overabundance of information, but the overconsumption of it that kills productivity."

As Hardy points out, our brains can focus on just so many things at one time. That's why having more than three goals at one time is confusing and doesn't allow you to focus on any one goal; inevitably, you wind up taking no action at all. Hardy says that having anything beyond three top goals drains your brain.

Certainly, people talk about the law of attraction, but Hardy says that they should really focus on the law of paying attention. "What you want or need has always been there, but now that you are paying attention, you are giving your brain the energy it needs to focus on it," he said. "You'll be able to isolate conversations and make connections to things you want, because now you are focused on it. Ideas will freely flow to you."

If you want to be an entrepreneur and push past your fears, you have to start paying laser-like attention to what you really want -- those top three goals -- and begin disregarding everything else.

What if you woke up tomorrow and read your obituary, announcing your death, online? How would that change your life? Would you be happy about all your accomplishments or regret not taking that one step that would have made all the difference in your life?

That very thing happened to Alfred Nobel. His brother had died, and the publication he read mistakenly said that *he* had died. From that day forward, he vowed to live a life of purpose. And today, the Nobel Prize, named in his honor, is one of the highest achievements there is. Nobel made that change in his life because he wanted *his* obituary to show something different. He applied laser-like focus to it. Will you do the same?

And there you have it. If you want to go deeper with me on this subject, sign up for my academy training here: http://bit.ly/MyFreeBonus

Chapter 30: Bonus: The Postage Stamp & The Morning Miracle

Consider the postage stamp. It wants to reach its destination as soon as postage stamply possible. ☺ But inevitably it knows there will be bumps along the road. Knowing this ahead of time, it prepares itself. How? By sticking to a set routine. It inches itself to the front of the mail processing line as early as possible. In the wee hours of the morning, when most people are still asleep, the postage stamp is doing its thing. It is traveling and bumping against other boxes, inching its way closer and closer to the delivery driver.

If you're this far along in the book, you are to be commended. I've just spent a lot of time talking to you about how to build your self-esteem and why delaying gratification will have success knocking on your door among other things. But in order to really get started, you need a system, a framework I dare say, that you can continually come back to when you feel down. It happens to the best of us. Remember, it's resistance at work. In the book, **_The War of Art_**, Steven Pressfield says "Resistance's goal is not to wound or disable. Resistance aims to kill. Its target is the epicenter of our being: our genius, our soul, the unique priceless gift we were put on earth to give and that no one else has but us. Resistance means business. When we fight it, we are in a war to the death."

Let me now introduce you to the Hal Elrod. I picked up his book, the **_Morning_**

Miracle a few years ago and it instantly resonated with me. I was already a morning person, routinely waking up at 4 a.m. in order to get my day started, but this gave me the framework and the continued inspiration I needed to keep it going.

In this interview with Navid Moazzez, https://www.youtube.com/watch?v=vITt DKlu1Gk

Hal Elrod shares his very inspiring story, and how the Miracle Morning is the not-so-obvious secret guaranteed to transform your life, and much, much more.

Do you want more for your life? Then you need to become better. The way you do that is with something you do every day. You must, like clockwork dedicate the time each day to becoming the person you need to be. *Instead of making a 'to do' list, you need to make a 'to become' list. You must 'be' before you can 'do' and you must 'do' before you can 'have'. "What's valuable in life is not what you get, but what you become," said Jim Rohn.*

Is resistance winning in your life?

I don't know you, but I'm going to say yes it is. How do I know this? Because it manifests itself in how you start your day. Consider the alarm on your phone. Every night you set it and every morning, you hit snooze. Now, let's give this some thought. The very first action of your day is to hit the snooze button. This may seem inconsequential, but is it really? Once again, it goes back to the word easy. It's easy to hit the snooze button and most do. But what people do not understand is that this action doesn't just affect that moment, it affects everything you do thereafter. The snooze button allows you to delay. Delay what? It allows you to delay, wait for it, your LIFE. By that one act, you are saying you prefer to remain unconscious in your life than to get up and create the life you want to live.

Have you ever heard of isolating incidents? This is when you mistakenly think that one thing you do does not affect any other thing you do. For example, *if you miss that early morning workout:*

- You'll probably procrastinate on that project
- Then, you'll most likely eat that fast food because you procrastinated
- Because you ate what you know you shouldn't, you need a little retail therapy, so you buy that item on credit

- You definitely won't drink 8 glasses of water this day because of all the sugary drinks you had at lunch
- You'll likely head back to the office and gossip about your friends/coworkers because you see them making progress and you're not
- When you get home, you'll scream at your kids because you're frustrated with yourself
- And finally when your mate gets home, you'll start an argument with him/her because you failed to keep your word to yourself to go for a workout. See how all that connects.

Stop deluding yourself. That one thing you skip, affects everything else. You must realize the real impact and consequence of each of our decisions. According to Elrod, every thought, choice and action is determining who you are becoming. In reality, he continues this type of action is programming your subconscious with the information that it is okay for you not to follow through with the things you've intended to do. Stop and think. The actions you take are bigger than just that action. It is determining the rest of your life.

How you wake up and how you start each day is vital to your levels of success in every area of your life. In the, _**The Morning Miracle**_, **Hal Elrod** says, "Focused, productive, successful mornings generate focused, productive, successful days – which inevitably create a successful life- in the same way that unfocused, unproductive and mediocre mornings generate unfocused, unproductive and mediocre days and ultimately a mediocre quality of life. By simply changing the way you wake up in the morning, you can transform any area of your life, faster than you ever thought possible."

Aren't you enthused by those words? I know I am. Yes, how you wake up and start your day can literally transform your life. Remember, when you start changing your habits, you are changing who you are becoming. Who you become is by far the greatest determinant in your quality of life now and in the future.

Yes, change is something most people avoid. That is why most people are overweight, in debt, depressed and lonely. This will not be you. High Point University President Nido Qubein said, "For the timid, change is frightening, for the comfortable, change is threatening, but for the confident, change is opportunity." This is your time, your opportunity to finally banish limiting thoughts and share with the world your gifts.

The framework that helped Hal Elrod can help you. He calls them Life S.A.V.E.R.S. They are six practices guaranteed to save you from an unfulfilled life.

The S stands for silence. He starts his day silently. Silence is one of the best ways to reduce stress and anxiety. During his silence he likes to meditate, pray, reflect, do some deep breathing and concentrate on gratitude.

The A stands for Affirmations. Elrod outlines in his book 5 simple steps to create your own affirmations.

#1 – What you really want – the purpose is to program your mind with beliefs, attitudes and behaviors that are vital to you being able to reach Level 10 success

#2 – Why you want it (deepest why's) – when you are clear, it will give you an unstoppable purpose

#3 – Whom you are committed to BEING to create it – things in life only get better when you do

#4 – What you're committed to DOING to attain it –if you want to write that book, you have to carve out time to actually write and then do it. Write it down and stick to it.

#5- Add Inspirational Quotes and Philosophies –whatever you read influences your thoughts. So pick your favorite motivational speaker, mine are Jim Rohn and Zig Ziglar and fill your mind with their thoughts.

The V stands for Visualization. The most successful athletes visualize. I like to call it intentional daydreaming. It enables you to see a future you want and when you do it enough, you will find ways to make it a reality. Visualization can be a powerful aid to overcoming self-limiting habits such as procrastination and to taking the actions necessary to achieve your goals.

The E stands for Exercise. Robin Sharma said, "If you don't make time for exercise, you'll probably have to make time for illness." I think you get the point.

Get moving. Just know that you will never feel like working out, but just remember, that emotion follows motion. So once you start moving you will feel good that you did.

The R stands for Reading. Mark Twain is quoted as saying, "A person who won't read has no advantage over one who can't read." You must develop a love for reading. Even if you don't like it, remember emotion follows motion. So just do it. If you really want Level 10 success, start reading. I've mentioned several books in this guide, why not pick one up?

The last S stands for Scribing, another way to put it would be journaling. I don't know about you, but whenever I get things out of my head and put them on paper, I see them more clearly. That is what journaling does. You gain mental clarity.

So you might be saying to yourself that all this would take too much time to do in the morning. Do you have at least six minutes in the morning? Then you have enough time to do all these things. Just take one minute for each.

Do it in 6 minutes

Minute 1… = Wake up, say a prayer of gratitude
Minute 2… Affirmations = your unlimited potential

Minute 3… Visualize = smiling and laughing with your mate

Minute 4… Write what you're Grateful for

Minute 5… Read a self-help book, a page or two

Minute6… Exercise – run for 60 seconds in place

"Discipline is the bridge between goals and accomplishments," says author Charles Duhigg in his book, *The Power of Habit: Why We Do What We Do in Life and Business.* That bridge must be crossed daily. Over time that daily crossing becomes a habit. Habits are behaviors that you repeat regularly and most often subconsciously. "People do not decide their future, they decide their habits and their habits decide their future." The key is consistency

Elrod says it takes at least 30 days to really solidify a habit. Unlike the pain and discomfort you experience in your first 20 days. In phase three, the transformation occurs. The new habit becomes a part of your identity. It transcends the space between something you're trying and who you are becoming In this phase also, you associate pleasure with your new habit.

Day 1 to 10 – Phase 1 – Unbearable
Day 11-20 – Phase 2 – Uncomfortable
Day 21- 30 – Phase 3 – Unstoppable

"Life begins at the end of your comfort zone," said Neale Donald Walsh. If you truly want to become the person you were meant to be, you have make the decision to commit now. Tomorrow does not exist.

In the book, *__The War of Art__,* **Steven Pressfield** says, "The moment one definitely commits oneself then providence comes. All sorts of things occur to help one that would not otherwise have occurred. This comes from the decision one makes. When we make a start and commit in the face of our fears, something wonderful happens. When we make a beginning, we get out of our own way and allow the universe to come in and do its job. The magic of doing: when we start, we are simply taking dictation, not really doing the work."

When you commit wonderful things happen.

The formula for failure is a few errors in judgment repeated every day according to Jim Rohn. Conversely, the formula for success is a few disciplines practiced every day. Eliminate the errors and replace it with practiced disciplines. When you do, you will never be the same. The people you love won't be the same either because when you get better, everyone in your life benefits.

In the end, it all comes down to this: "If you were meant to cure cancer or write a screenplay and you don't, you not only hurt yourself, even destroy yourself. You hurt your children. You hurt me. You hurt the planet. You shame the angels who watch over you and you spite the Almighty who created you and only you with your unique gifts, for the sole purpose of nudging the human race one millimeter farther along its path back to God. Creative work is not selfish. It's a gift to the world and every being in it. Don't cheat us of your contribution. Give us what you've got," says Pressfield in his book, *__The War of Art.__*

So I end this book the way I began. Give us what you got. Continue to press on. You got this. Along this road, called life, never ever give up. Remember to live life more like a postage stamp!

And there you have it. If you want to go deeper with me on this subject, sign up for my academy training here: http://bit.ly/MyFreeBonus

Chapter 31: The Postage Stamp & Companies

Consider the postage stamp. It always goes above and beyond to produce the best possible outcome for its recipient. Whatever road it has to travel to reach you the fastest, it will take it. It will always continue to innovate and get better and better. Before, postage stamps had to be licked in order to stick to a letter. But because of innovation and an attention to detail, the postage stamp is now self-adhesive. The postage stamp has a core belief of excellence, commitment and continuous improvement, much like the following companies.

Amazon – Founded in 1994 in the garage of Jeff Bezos, Amazon continues to innovate and has become the go-to online store for the world. Jeff embodies the ideals of the postage stamp. He left a high-paying job in New York and embarked on this unknown start-up. He never ever gave up. He persevered. Like a farmer, he kept sowing and now he is very happily reaping the fruits of his hard labor. Thank you, Jeff.

Apple – Who doesn't love every Apple product? A huge thank you to Steve Jobs and Steve Wozniak for their non-negotiable devotion to improving the connectivity of our lives. The iPhone and later iPad have continued to revolutionize the way we connect with one another. Their combined attention to detail and their never ever give up spirit has helped shaped American culture. Thank you both for always continuing to hone your skill set because we are the recipients of your hard work. We miss you Steve Jobs. Thank you Tim Cook for your current leadership and vision, can't wait to see what the future holds.

Airbnb – Thank you Brian Chesky, Joe Gebbia and Nathan Blecharczyk for disrupting the hotel industry. This venture is one of the most ingenious and one I have used several times. Thank you for not giving up. You did not allow a lack of capital to stop you. You developed a special edition breakfast cereal to help generate the necessary funds and the rest is history.

FaceBook – Thank you Mark Zuckerberg for practicing relentlessly in private when it came to honing your skills as a programmer. You stick-to-itiveness allowed you to eventually connect the planet with Facebook. Just like the postage stamp, you stuck to your goals and we are the benefactors. You never ever gave up and for that we applaud you.

Google – Thank you Larry Page and Sergey Brin for not giving up on your dream. While they were students, the two founded Google in 1998. They could have given up, but they did not. They stuck to their goal and today we are better for it. The internet already had search engines, but they had an idea and they stuck to it. They took massive action and made Google a household name.

LinkedIn – Thank you Reid Hoffman and the many other founding team members for not giving up. LinkedIn is a tool I use almost every day to write about topics important to me and to grow my network professionally. You truly embody what your book, *The Start-Up of You* espouses, which is the need to become the CEO of your own career. Thanks so much Reid.

Hilton Hotels & Resorts – Thank you Conrad Hilton for not giving up when as a young man you intended to purchase a bank, but when that fell through, you purchased a hotel instead. We are all happy that you did. Whenever I travel on business, my first chose of hotel is Hilton. Every one that I've been to has been five-stars. Thank you for leaving such a great legacy.

Papyrus – I don't know about you, but I love paper and cards. Thank you Marcel and Margrit Schurman for not giving up on your dream. You have introduced the world to fine art we can hold in the palm of our hands. The beautiful quality and craftsmanship of your products are without compare. We wholeheartedly appreciate you sticking to your dream.

Bombas – Thank you Randy Goldberg and David Heath for giving away more than 1 million socks to those in need. I did not know that socks were the #1 most requested item among the homeless. You heard that quote and both of you went to work and made it your mission to help and serve. We applaud you.

Starbucks – I'm not an avid coffee drinker, but I love the occasional Caramel Frappuccino. Thank you to the founding members and especially Howard Schultz for making Starbucks what it is today. Not only can individuals get refreshing beverages, it is also a place to gather and meet and enjoy the company of others. Thank you for never ever giving up and for continuing to innovate and be philanthropic.

Jamba, Inc. – After I started getting up and going to the gym at 5 a.m. I also started juicing. When I didn't have time to juice, I would frequent Jamba Juice. Today, I still do. Thanks Jamba for your amazing juices.

PayPal – Thank you Max Levchin, Peter Thiel, Luke Nosek and Ken Howery for sticking to your dreams of creating this amazing money transfer service. I don't know anyone who hasn't used Paypal. It is a great way to receive and send money. Thanks for not giving up and for making it easier to do business online.

Stripe – Thank you John and Patrick Collison for developing this awesome online payment system. Your system really helps us entrepreneurs focus on what we do best which is create and we can leave the payment collection to you.

Pixar – Thanks Edwin Catmull and Alvy Ray Smith for your amazing computer animation skills. I absolutely loved *Ratatouille* and *Inside Out*. Thanks to you both and to your staff for the constant joy and laughter you bring into all of our lives. A special thanks also to Jim Morris and John Lasseter.

Simon & Schuster – I have been an avid reader and writer my entire life and I have always wanted my book to be published by your company. I hold that as a goal in my mind and I know one day it will come true. Thanks Richard Simon and Max Schuster.

Stamps.com – This is by far the best and fastest way to purchase stamps online. I love your PhotoStamps. Thanks Jim McDermott, Ari Engelberg and Jeff Green for working hard while still students at UCLA and never giving up.

The Smithsonian – Thank you for your 19 world-class museums, galleries, garden and zoo. Being able to freely learn about history is a glorious gift. The Haupt Garden is simply breathtaking and provides a sort of horticultural therapy as you walk by under the seductive blue sky. My favorite two museums are the African American Museum and the Postal Museum. Thank you to everyone who works so hard to keep these masterpieces in pristine condition.

Uber – Thank you Travis Kalanick and Garrett Camp for disrupting the transportation industry and for contributing to the You Economy. I personally use the service and have worked as a driver. Thank you for not giving up and for helping all of us reach our next destination safely. We are all so happy you had trouble getting a cab in Paris. That trouble led to the company we use every single day.

Lyft – Thank you Logan Green and John Zimmer for providing healthy competition in this ride-sharing industry. I also use your service and have worked for your company as well. Thanks for travelling to Zimbabwe and getting inspired to create this amazing company, for taking the risk, for meeting each other on Facebook initially and for providing exquisite customer service.

Verizon – I just want to say I have always had the most reliable service as a customer. Thank you for always being there when I needed to speak to my mom when she was still alive. I taught her how to text and that became our go-to tool for communication. Thank you for Verizon for continuing to improve your telecommunications network. I can hear you now.

Xfinity – Talk about lightning fast internet service. Thank you for continuing to raise the bar.

AAA - As a single woman, I just want to say thank you for your great and reliable service. Whenever I have had a flat tire, I always call and a technician is sent out immediately. Your employees are kind and helpful. Thanks for the stellar service.

Farmers Insurance Group – I have been a loyal customer for many years and I just want to thank John Tyler and Thomas Leavey for founding the company. I'm an excellent driver so I have not needed to contact your company, but knowing you are there is comforting.

Ontraport – Thanks Landon Ray, Pin Chen and Steven Schneider for helping to make the life of an entrepreneur online a tad bit easier. Thanks for sticking it out in the early days. It really has paid off and we all reap the benefits.

Fitbit Inc. – Thank you James Park and Eric Friedman. I use my Fitbit every single day. One of the things that really helped me overcome my depression was walking. I love counting my steps. It encourages me to remain active all throughout the day. Thanks for such a great product.

Zoom – Thank you Eric Yuan for never giving up. When you applied for a visa to come to the United States from China, you were denied eight times, but you kept trying and on your ninth try, you were successful. You could not speak English when you first arrived, but you persisted. I applaud your "never ever give up spirit." Thank you Eric for Zoom, it is the best platform I've used for video conferencing. It is my go-to choice.

Zapier – Thank you Wade Foster, Bryan Helmig and Mike Knoop for creating your software. It's the best task automation software out there. I don't exactly understand how the app does what it does, but thank you.

Kajabi – Thank you Kenny Rueter and Travis Rosser for creating your amazing platform. I am a proud customer. Thanks for your hard work and for continuing to innovate and introduce new products to Kajabi.

Ecamm Network – Thanks Ken and Glen Aspeslagh for creating great products for consumers. I love your new Ecamm Live for Facebook. Keep the great products coming.

Get Stencil – Thanks Adam Rotman and Oliver Nassar for creating this get service to make images. This is my number one go-to website for easily creating an image for a blog post or other social media. Thanks for not giving up.

Leadpages – Thank you Clay Collins and Tracy Simmons for creating your software. It truly makes being an entrepreneur a whole lot easier. With your software I am tech savvy and it helps me to help other people by getting my message out there. Thank again for sticking to your vision and not giving up.

Techsmith – Thanks William Hamilton for co-creating such a great software company. I use Camtasia all the time and I love Snagit. Thanks for not giving up and for pivoting from consulting to a software company.

Airlines:

Southwest – Thank you Southwest for your low-fares and the opportunity to choose your own seats. Whenever I fly, your airline is my first choice. The staff is always nice and courteous. A special thanks to founders Rollin King and Herbert Kelleher.

JetBlue Airways & Azul Brazilian Airlines – Obrigada (Thank you) David Neeleman for creating JetBlue and Azul. I learned Portuguese and I am a frequent visitor to Brazil. Thanks for allowing all your passengers to have great flying experiences.

Healthcare:

Kaiser Permanente – In a nutshell, I love your tagline, Thrive. I believe taking care of your health is essential. Thank you for the reminder.

Sharp Healthcare – I had to have surgery a few years ago while living in San Diego and Sharp Healthcare was absolutely amazing. The nurses were phenomenal. I received the best care I could have ever dreamed of. Thank you all.

Auto:

Ford Motor Company – A special thanks to Henry Ford. He had a vision and would not stop until it became a reality. He stuck to his goal the way a postage stamp sticks to a letter. Words cannot adequately express how Ford galvanized the automotive industry. Ford never gave up and he founded the company at 39 years old. Throughout the years since, Ford has experienced some financial setbacks, but the company has never given up and they are a force to be reckoned with today.

Tesla – Thank you Elon Musk for being an avid reader. I believe books are one of the best ways to learn how to improve our lives. Thank you for not giving up when you were bullied in school. You exemplify the postage stamp and you've stuck to your vision to change the world whether it be on this planet with your cars or in another galaxy in space. Thank you for continuing to inspire us to never ever give up in our pursuit for excellence.

Toyota Motor Corporation – I have driven a Toyota for most of my adult life. Thank you Kiichiro Toyoda for creating such a reliable and dependable car. Thanks Toyota for such a great car.

BMW – Simply put, I just love this car. It is so beautifully designed. Thank you Franz Josep Popp, Karl Rapp, Camillo Castiglioni. Your BMW X5 is a work of genius. This is my dream car. Thank you for designing my dream.

Enterprise Rent-A-Car – Thanks Jack Taylor for creating this brand. Whenever I need to rent a car, the men and women I encounter at Enterprise are exceptional. Thank you for your great customer service.

Food:

Rubio's Restaurants, Inc. – Thanks Ralph Rubio for your regular pilgrimages to Mexico where you became hooked on the fish taco. I'm glad you did, because I love Rubio's. I love your fresh, high quality ingredients and food. Thanks for not giving up.

Chipotle Mexican Grill, Inc. – Thanks for your commitment to the best ingredients and respect for animals, to the farmers and our environment. I love your food. Thanks for making it available.

Pieology - Thanks Carl Chang for creating Pieology. I love the fact that you can choose the ingredients you want on your pizza and that you can see it being cooked. It is truly a celebration of food.

Chick-Fil-A- Thank you S.Truett Cathy for standing by your strong religious beliefs and going against the norm by closing all your restaurants every Sunday so that families could worship and spend time together. Also, thank you for creating the best chicken sandwich known to man.

McDonalds – Thank you to the McDonald brothers and Ray Kroc for epitomizing what it means to never ever give up. The McDonald brothers began McDonalds as a barbeque restaurant, but later pivoted and turned it into a hamburger stand. Enterprising entrepreneur Ray Kroc purchased the chain in the 1950's and it's still going strong. Also, thank you for creating the best French fries known to man.

Pepsi-Cola Company – I love your Performance with Purpose efforts to create a healthier relationship between people and food. You are actively involved in reducing added sugars and saturated salts while increasing your emphasis on positive nutrition. Thank you.

Coca-Cola Company – Thank you for creating great brands such as Odwalla. I absolutely love this smoothie. Thanks for also giving back to the community and for helping others through The Coca-Cola Foundation.

Water.org – Clean drinking water is essential to life. Thanks Gary White and Matt Damon for creating this organization and helping with the global water crisis.

Charity: Water – Thank you Scott Harrison for bringing attention to the global crisis of unsafe drinking water. Thank you for never giving up and for "putting on charity" as it states in Colossians 3:14.

Instacart – Thanks Apoorva Mehta, Max Mullen and Brandon Leonardo for this great grocery-delivery service. Sometimes you just need that one or two ingredients to make that awesome dinner and you can't leave the kitchen to go to the store. Thanks for not giving up.

Retail:

Hobbs London – Wow, thank you so much for your amazing fashions. It is oftentimes really difficult to find modest yet fashionable apparel, but your brand bring the two seamlessly together. A special thanks to founders Yoram and Marilyn Anselm and current CEO Meg Lustman. I think of your company as a postage stamp because you refuse to stop innovating and creating great styles for women.

Macy's – Thank you Rowland H. Macy for not giving up when your first four attempts in the retail business failed. You learned from your failures and went on to create one of the most renowned retail stores the world has ever known. We admire your tenacity and determined spirit. Thank you for your postage-like qualities.

Walmart – Thank you Samuel M. Walton for creating an economical place to shop and for not giving up on your dreams. Even when you faced obstacles as you opened your first store in Arkansas, you were supported by your lovely wife, Helen and your father-in-law, which is necessary when embarking on a new adventure. You never ever gave up and all the customers who shop every day at Walmart and Sam's Club are better for it.

Costco Wholesale Corporation – Thank you James Sinegal and Jeffrey Brotman for creating Costco. This is my go-to place for shopping. I love to buy things in bulk because it lasts for such a long time. Thanks also for your affordable gas prices. I am happy to be customer. Thanks for your commitment to excellence.

Banking:

Wells Fargo – I really admire Wells Fargo and their CEO Timothy J. Sloan for their commitment to restore trust in their brand. Sloan took the helm at a critical time in the company's history. But Wells Fargo is determined to regain the confidence of its employees as well as the public. Their marketing campaign is focused on Building Better Every Day. Even though this is not a favorable time for the company, they are resolved to not give up in resolving this problem. They are well aware of the mistakes they made and are continuously working to improve and make things better than they were before.

Golden 1 Credit Union – I believe credit unions are essential. Since I moved to Sacramento, I have been a member of Golden 1 Credit Union and I absolutely love it. Credit Unions are not-for-profit organizations that exist to serve their members. President and CEO Donna Bland has more than 20 years of experience in financial services and Golden 1 continues to thrive under her oversight and commitment to excellence.

Universities:

University of Southern California – I was accepted at USC in the fall of 1992. It was the only school I ever wanted to attend. I had to withdraw from USC in the first semester because my mom was diagnosed with ovarian cancer and I had to get a full-time job. I will always consider it my alma mater, even though I didn't get a chance to graduate. I want to thank the professors and staff at USC. This institution continues to be a recognized leader in education, innovation and philanthropy.

Sacramento State – I've only lived in Sacramento for a few years now, but I love it. It is truly a great place to work and live. I've discovered that Sacramento State has enjoyed a rich history as a center of higher learning since 1947. They began in rented rooms, but now they are a regional powerhouse. Plans are in the works to expand and transform the campus into a multi-dimensional, state-of-the-art, cutting-edge institution. Sacramento State students and alumni are proud to "Made at Sac State."

University of California, Davis – I love the city of Davis, CA. It is so quaint. Every street seems like its tree-lined and the vibe is just so chill. Right in the middle is UC Davis. The campus is beautiful and almost every person you see is riding a bicycle. Thank you UC

Davis for such an immaculate college and calming surroundings.

Magazines:

Black Enterprise Magazine – Thank you Earl G. Graves Sr. for creating a newsletter about economic development and urban affairs that would one day become the magazine we know today. This magazine is one of my favorites. Your son is doing an excellent job as CEO. He wrote one of the most touches letters in the magazine when his mom, your wife died. Your family is forever in my prayers. Thank you for all that you do.

Success Magazine – I have been a subscriber to Success Magazine for years and I want to thank everyone who has worked at this company. I became a reader when Darren Hardy was at the helm and I simply loved receiving the CDs every month in the magazine. I still have every CD. But now things are digital and I listen to the interviews on the Success Talks podcast. Thank you for your continued commitment to expanding our knowledge about personal development and the great online training you are providing with Brendon Burchard.

Local Sacramento Businesses:

FoodJets – Thank you Darren McAdams for launching this company. This Sacramento-based local food delivery service is great. I've worked as an independent contractor and the company really is terrific. FoodJets stopped taking orders for a while until McAdams revamped it, but now it is going full steam ahead. Thank you for not giving up and for creating local jobs for city's residents.

Quick Quack Car Wash – I love this car wash company, thank you Jason Johnson for founding the company. Each week when I get my car washed at various locations in Sacramento, I am greeted by a very friendly staff. I especially love the unlimited car washes you can get every month and the free vacuum for the inside of your car.

And there you have it. There are many more companies that pattern themselves after the postage stamp, but space would not permit me to list them all.

Be sure to sign up for my Free Academy Training (just in case you missed all the other times to sign up) http://bit.ly/MyFreeBonus

Chapter 32: The Postage Stamp & My Mentors

Consider the postage stamp. Its main purpose is to help your letter or package reach its intended destination. At its core the postage is a helper. The following people have helped me in some way by their message, good example or their never ever give up spirit. Mentors or helpers are needed in every area of life. I would like to thank the following people, none of whom I have ever met.

Jim Rohn – Thank you Jim for your mentorship. Though I never got a chance to meet you, I hear you almost daily when I commute to work. Your words and philosophy continue to inspire me each and every day.

Zig Ziglar – Thank you Zig for your mentorship as well. I never got a chance to meet you, but your audio tapes were my first introduction to my personal development. Thank you for your great stories, sharing your life with the public and for never ever giving up.

Brian Tracy – I've read many of your books and I want to thank you for your personal dedication to self-improvement. I reread your books all the time and I always find something new in it each time. Thank you so much for helping people like me.

Jack Canfield - I read your book, *The Success Principles* over 10 years ago and I still refer to it today. The wisdom you dispensed in that book is timeless. Reading this book feels like you are holding me by the hand and helping me get better and better. Thank you.

Tony Robbins – Thanks Tony for your constant encouragement. I have listened to your audio tapes for many years. While living in Los Angeles, I go an opportunity to hear you speak in person and it was to say the least, moving and transformative. Thanks for not giving up along the way. Your example has helped so many people, including me.

George Lucas – I applaud you for not giving up on your vision to let art be freely available to all. Your museum will create a true cultural awareness for the art of visual storytelling. This will truly be a full-circle moment for you in that your museum will be housed near the very film school (USC) you attended. Well done.

Warren Buffet – You are to be commended for looking fear in the face and winning. You were once afraid to speak in public; in fact, you arranged your life so that you wouldn't have to.

But, you knew it was something that you had to overcome so you enrolled in a Dale Carnegie course and the rest is history. Thank you for sharing that side of yourself and for helping the rest of us see that if we don't give up we too, can succeed.

Denzel Washington – In a speech in which you won the Image Award for Outstanding Actor, you said, "Without commitment you will never start and without consistency you will never finish." Thank you for your commitment and consistency in perfecting your craft. And thank you for also telling us that, "Ease is a greater threat to progress than hardship." Thank you for never ever giving up and for not taking it easy.

Magic Johnson – When I think of the Lakers, you are the first person that comes to mind. Having been born and raised in Los Angeles, I can remember watching the games with my family. It was a treat to see you play. Thank you for so many great memories. I am not surprised that now you are the president of basketball operations of the Los

Angeles Lakers. Keep up the good work Magic, we really appreciate you.

Jamie Foxx – I want to thank your grandmother, Miss Talley. All of us need someone that believes in us and she was that person for you. I am so happy she made you take piano lessons, because you play beautifully. I read that you still practice the piano for two hours many days. Thanks for your self-discipline and for continuing to hone your craft.

Misty Copeland – In reading your book, *Life In Motion*, I really got to know you as a person. Thanks for being so open and vulnerable about your life and the struggles you endured. Even though you moved around a lot, ballet was always a constant in your life and you never gave up. Congratulations on all your success.

Nido Qubein – There is one quote of yours that has always resonated with me and still inspires me to this day. "For the timid, change is frightening; for the comfortable, change is threatening; but for the confident change is opportunity."

This quote always makes me examine my actions to ensure that I act with courage and confidence in everything I do.

Simon Cowell – I love your honesty and candor. In life we may not always want to hear the truth, but it's something we need to hear. Whenever you judged a singing competition, I felt that your criticism came from a place of love and of wanting to help rather than to hurt.

David Hornik – The first word that comes to mind when I think of David is generous. He is a venture capitalist with August Capital. He gives entrepreneurs a chance to present ideas to him and if he's intrigued, he backs the deal with his own money. Even if he doesn't give them money, he tries to help these new business owners by sharing his knowledge. He also personally responds to emails from complete strangers (indeed, he replied to me). He's happy to help even if he won't financially benefit from a transaction. For him, giving is his default weapon of choice. Thank you for your generosity.

Ryan Levesque – When I read your book, *Ask,* the part that stood out to me the most was the letter you wrote your mom. My mom was my best friend so when I read that I literally cried. I also loved how you were so determined to learn Chinese that nothing was going to stand in your way. The story of when you went back to school and spoke to your professor in Chinese is nothing short of amazing and inspirational. Thanks Ryan for not giving up.

Pat Flynn – Thanks Pat for your generosity in sharing what you know about creating Smart Passive Income (the same name as your website). You were one of the first persons I came across online that was honest and completely transparent about online business. Thanks for what you do to help others.

Tim Ferriss - Thanks for your book, The 4-Hour Work Week. I was in the bookstore one day when I came across this very intriguing title. I picked it up and it has served as constant inspiration. Thanks for sharing your knowledge and for not giving up along the way.

Scooter Braun – I loved your recent interview on Success Talks about vulnerability and the need to embrace that one day things may come to an end. Your love for your family is a beautiful thing to see and I applaud you for scheduling time in your day to play with your kids. Thanks for not giving up on your dreams.

Kobe Bryant – Thank you for your tireless work ethic. I loved your speech after you were bestowed the Espy Icon Award. You said that you were being honored because you had a dream and you let nothing stand in your way. Thank you for all the days you got up at 4 a.m. and practiced relentlessly in private. You truly embody the words of your English teacher who said, "Rest at the end and not in the middle." Thank you for teaching us that in order to have true success we must first make a commitment to ourselves and never ever give up. We look forward to how you will continue to inspire us all in the future, because as you said, "This is not the end for me."

LeBron James – I really admire your love for the city of Cleveland. You left in order to get a championship ring and many people, to put it mildly, were not happy with your "decision." I supported your decision, because all of us have the right to choose where we want to work. But what is so remarkable is that you came back to that city that spoke so unkindly of you and not only did you come back; you won a championship for that city. Thanks for your stellar example.

Bill & Melinda Gates – Thank you Bill and Melinda for the work you do at your foundation. Thank you for showing how much you care about humanity. Thank you for embodying the spirit of The Golden Rule.

DeVon Frankline & Meagan Good – I just want to say thank you for your book, *The Wait.* I applaud both of you for living by Bible standards and choosing to wait until marriage to have sex. I believe when you can exercise self-control in this area, then there is nothing you can't do in life. Thank you both for your candor and honesty.

Venus & Serena Williams – I love tennis. You two make the sport so exciting and dynamic. I remember seeing you on TV when you were little girls practicing. All that hard work paid off. I love to watch you play doubles. Thanks for the inspiration.

Daymond John – I want to first thank your mother for teaching you how to sew and for always believing in your dream. Mothers are priceless. Thank you for not giving up and for creating your clothing company FUBU. Thank you for your book, *The Power of Broke*. It helped us to see that when you've got nothing to lose, then you've got everything to gain.

Dave Ramsey – Thanks for your great money advice in your book, The Total Money Makeover. I love your motto that says, "If you will live like no one else, later you can live like no one else."

Basically, if we make sacrifices now that most people aren't willing to make, later on we will be able to live like others never will be able to. I also love your Debt Snowball Tool. Thanks again.

Reed Hastings – What I love about your story is that you encountered a problem as it related to late fees imposed on DVD rentals and from that you had an idea to eliminate that problem, you acted on that idea and today we have NETFLIX. You had a vision and no matter what you kept at it. You did not give up.

Adele – I love that you act in the face of your fears. I've heard you say that you still get physically ill when you have to perform in front of a crowd, and yet you don't let fear win. Thank you for your beautiful voice and for sharing it with the world even though it may not always be easy to do so.

Amy Porterfield - Thank you for being the consummate professional that you are. I became your online student in 2017 and I have literally devoured everything you've taught. Thank you so much for your hard work and attention to deal. I love your podcast, *Online Marketing Made Easy*.

Taylor Swift – I really admire how you knew what you wanted to do at a young age and you went after it. I love your how you write from your heart and perform songs that we all can relate to. You also have a fierce loyalty for all your fans. Thanks Taylor.

Sade - I love your music and your style. There is no other singer out there like you. Your music is classic and ethereal. Thank you for sharing your voice with the world.

Celine Dion – Wow, your voice is simply amazing. Thank you so much for sharing your incredible gift with the world. Your songs have uplifted me and inspired me to keep going. I am so very sorry for the loss of your husband. Your love for him was a beautiful thing to be a witness to.

Sara Blakely – Thank you for not giving on your dream to make better undergarments for women. I admire that you refused to take no for answer when you first started out with Spanx. No one saw your vision, but you did. You encourage all of us to never to stop trying and to chase after our dreams.

Bo Eason – This former NFL player helps you realize the power of your personal story. Thank you for your amazing and heartfelt YouTube videos that show us how we all can become better storytellers. You are a master communicator and your heart and sincerity are palpable. Thank you for not giving up on your journey.

Russell Wilson – I would like to thank your dad for instilling in you the, "why not you" attitude. Thanks for motivating young people today to do their best. Everyone needs a helping hand. Thanks for extending yours.

Lisa Price – I love the name of your company, Carol's Daughter. It not only pays homage to your mom but embodies the woman you are today. Thanks Lisa, for not giving up and for testing out new products and continuing to listen to want consumers want and providing it.

Shonda Rhimes – I love that you love to write. Thank you for your candor and for being so open, honest and vulnerable in your book, Year of Yes. Thanks for the Wonder Woman pose tip to help increase your confidence, love it, who knew? Thanks for never ever giving up.

Tyler Perry – I miss you and Madea. Thanks Tyler for never giving up on your dream, no matter how hard it got. I heard you give an interview once and you said the key to success is to focus on one thing. That advice has helped me so much. As entrepreneurs it's easy to get distracted, but now, I have a singular focus. Lastly, thanks for opening up about the abuse you experienced as young man. That was so courageous and has helped so many of us to soldier on because things do get better.

Oprah Winfrey – I love your quote which says, "Turn your wounds into wisdom." That is exactly what I set out to do with this book. Thank you for providing a sterling example. Your wisdom has touched so many people in so many ways that I just want to say thank you from all of us.

And there you have it. There are many more people I admire for their postage-stamp like qualities, but space would not permit me to list them all.

Be sure sign up for my Free Academy Training here: http://bit.ly/MyFreeBonus

Chapter 33: The Postage Stamp & Cities

Compton, CA – With the help of many supporters such as Dr. Dre, Compton is well on its way to becoming a leader in education. The new Compton High School project will truly be transformational for the students and families living there. A thank you goes to the Compton Unified School District.

Another round of applause goes to Dr. Dre for donating $10 million dollars to help fund this initiative. The Compton community will now have unrestricted access to opportunity. Thank you for not giving up.

Detroit, MI – We have all heard about the woes of Detroit. But Detroit is showing the world that it will not be counted it. Every day they are making major strides to take this city back to the heights it enjoyed during the reign of the big three auto manufacturers. Thank you to all residents in Detroit and the men and women who refuse to give up.

And there you have it. There are many more cities, but once again space and time would not permit me to list them all.

Be sure to sign up for my Free Academy Training here: http://bit.ly/MyFreeBonus

Chapter 34: The Postage Stamp & Young People

Consider the postage stamp. It never ever gives up.

I don't know you personally, but I do know you are an extraordinary person. How do I know? Well, do you remember what I talked about in chapter 26, if you forgot, please reread this:

In a talk at TEDx San Francisco, Mel Robbins, self-help author of the book, *The 5 Second Rule*, mentioned that scientists estimate the probability of your being born at about one in 400 trillion.

Do you know what that means?

It means you are engineered for success and designed to have high levels of self-esteem, self-respect and personal pride. You are extraordinary. There has never been anyone exactly like you in all history of mankind on the earth. You have amazing untapped talents and abilities that, when properly directed and applied, can bring you everything you could ever want or dream of.

Don't ever forget that.

When times get tough, as they most definitely will, because of the world we live in; remember that no bad situation will last forever. What you are experiencing is temporary and things will get better. If you are being verbally, physically or sexually abused talk to a trusted adult.

Confide in your parents, a teacher or another responsible adult about how you feel and get the help you need in order to not give up on yourself or on life. Talking about your feelings may not be easy, but, believe me, it is the best thing to do. Granted, your problems won't disappear just because you are talking about them. But the support of a trusted confidant may be just what you need to put your situation in perspective.

Also, don't forget the adage, "There is more happiness in giving, than there is in receiving." Basically, this means that when you help others, you also help yourself. When you unselfishly help someone in need, it takes your mind off your problems and you feel better because you helped someone. So be generous with your time. Can you help your parents or grandparents or someone else? Make a list and then go help them. You will feel amazing afterwards.

Above all remember your true value. You are a masterpiece, one-of-a-kind. There is no one on earth exactly like you. You are a work of art, just like the Mona Lisa. Please talk to an adult if you are experiencing overwhelming problems. Confide in someone you can trust.

And there you have it. Be sure to sign up for my Free Academy Training here: http://bit.ly/MyFreeBonus

Chapter 35: The Postage Stamp & You

So there you have it. I hope this information has served you. I sincerely appreciate you taking the time to read my book.

Now the ball is in your court. What will you do with the information you just read?

My intention is for you to continue to skyrocket your self-confidence, continue implementing bullet-proof habits and ultimately achieve all of your goals.

What I would like for you to do is to go out and buy your favorite book of stamps and keep it in your wallet or purse and whenever you feel you can't do something, take out the stamp and ponder over its purpose.

If you want me to help you do that, please sign up for my free Masterclass. In the Masterclass I go over *How to Master Your Mindset, Make Money Online and Succeed in every area of your life.*

http://bit.ly/MyFreeBonus

May I ask a favor?

If you've benefited from this book or have found it useful in any way, would you mind writing a short review on Amazon. You can use this link: http://amzn.to/2t7e2aH

I want to thank you from the bottom of my heart for your support.

And I want to say a final thank you to the hard-working men and women who work at the U.S. Postal Service. We are the original social network. Thank you for entrusting us with your mail. We are proud to deliver for you!

Until we meet again.

Meiko S. Patton

And there you have it. Be sure to sign up for my Free Academy Training here: http://bit.ly/MyFreeBonus

About Meiko S. Patton

In 2008, while employed by the U.S. Postal Service as a Letter Carrier in Los Angeles, Meiko's life was served a devastating blow when her 59-year-old mom was diagnosed and later died from Stage IV colon and liver cancer. After her mom's death, Meiko spiraled into a deep depression.

One day, while contemplating suicide, the thought of a postage stamp popped into her mind. That thought saved her life. That was nearly 10 years ago.

Today, Meiko is an Amazon #1 Best-Selling Author of How a Postage Stamp Saved My Life **and Founder of Never Ever Give Up Academy.**

Meiko helps entrepreneurs skyrocket their self-confidence so that they can begin working on that new product or online course they've been thinking about. She believes the best way to gain confidence in any area is to take massive action by first writing a book.

She also helps federal employees shrink their fears and encourages them to achieve their financial goals outside of their 9 to 5 careers, because you'll never know when another government shutdown might occur.

In addition, Meiko helps individuals dealing with recurring negative thoughts to learn how to harness their habits so that they can finally live the life they want.

Meiko's work can be seen on Entrepreneur.com, Huffington Post, Life Hack,
BlogHer, Govloop.com Fedsmith.com, Careers in Government and Postal Posts.

Meiko loves to travel, run marathons, volunteer in her community, count her steps with Fitbit and learn new languages.

And yes, Meiko, still works for the U.S. Postal Service in their Sacramento district office.

Meiko has lived in Los Angeles, CA, San Diego, CA, and she currently resides in Sacramento, CA.

YouTube:
https://www.youtube.com/c/MeikoPatton

Periscope: @careersavvyfed (Meiko S. Patton)

Facebook Fan Page:
https://www.Facebook.com/MeikoPatton

Twitter: @careersavvyfed

Google +:
https://plus.google.com/+MeikoPatton

Pinterest:
https://www.pinterest.com/meikopatton/

Instagram:
https://www.instagram.com/meikopatton

LinkedIn:
https://www.linkedin.com/in/meikopatton/

Website: https://meiko-patton-398b.mykajabi.com/

Blog: https://meiko-patton-398b.mykajabi.com/blog

Other Books by Meiko S. Patton

The Giant Strawberry is a children's book that was written by Meiko in 2006. The idea came from a story her mom made up to entertain her eight brothers and sisters when they were little kids. http://amzn.to/2t7e2aH

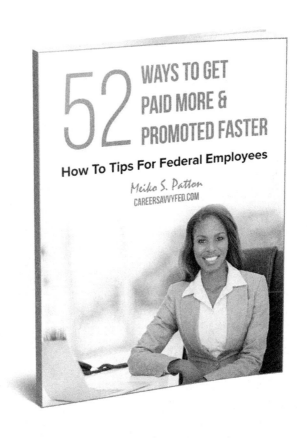

52 Ways to Get Paid More & Promoted Faster is a how-to book for Federal Employees.
http://amzn.to/2t7e2aH

Teach Online: How to Create Side Hustle Income Leveraging Your Existing Skills. http://amzn.to/2t7e2aH

21 Ways to Achieve Wealth & Success. This book is based on my wildly successful Entrepreneur.com article.
http://amzn.to/2t7e2aH

Products by Meiko S. Patton

Master Your Mindset Course

If you liked the book and want to go deeper with me on these topics and get more insight into how you can achieve your goals through positive thought patterns, then please join me in my online course.

In this 21-day course, you will not only Master Your Mindset, you will also write your 10-chapter life legacy book. I believe all of us have a book inside us and when we tap into our inner wisdom and put it on paper, your self-confidence will skyrocket. It did for me!

Book Meiko to Speak!

Book Meiko S. Patton to speak at your next event and your audience will not only thank you, but they will be motivated and inspired to take immediate action!

For over a decade, Meiko S. Patton has been educating, motivating and inspiring business owners, entrepreneurs, consultants and employees to not only start their own businesses, but to develop the right positive mindset needed to sustain success.

When Meiko's mom died, she wanted to die as well, but the thought of a postage stamp helped change her mind. Meiko is compassionate and sympathetic to people who deal with recurring negative thoughts and she is well-equipped to help provide the skills needed to forge ahead.

She believes that writing is a form of therapy and that all of us have a book inside us. She knows first-hand that writing a Life Legacy Book can be transformative and one of the best ways to boost your self-confidence and elevate your self-image and self-esteem.

Meiko's most requested signature talks are:

- **How a Postage Stamp Can Save Your Life Keynote Speech for Your Employees, Young People or Your Organization**
- **Lacking in Confidence? 10 Reasons Why You Need to Write a Book Today**
- **How to Earn Side-Hustle Income Teaching What You Already Know While Working Your 9-to-5 Job**
- **The Best Way to Truly Engage Your Employees**

For more information and to book Meiko for your next event, send her an email at: meikopatton@gmail.com

Mommy, I will see you in the resurrection. Love, Meiko

- John 11:25

Printed in Great Britain
by Amazon

18920591R00149